THE LAST DAYS

The Last Days

LOWER CHEDWORTH

1940 – 1959

Barry Pilkington

Illustrations by Barry Pilkington
Poem 'Steps' by Martin Kilby

Cover image
'Cotswold Stones at Lower Chedworth'
(Pancake Hill)
Alan Gosset James c.1935
(Exhibited at the 87th Exhibition of the
New English Art Club at Cheltenham Art Gallery, August 1936)
Copyright © 2018 Christie's Images Limited

Extract from Laurie Lee – *Cider With Rosie*.
Reproduced with permission of Curtis Brown Group Ltd,
on behalf of the beneficiaries of the Estate of Laurie Lee.
Copyright © Laurie Lee 1959

Matador
9 Priory Business Park,
Wistow Road, Kibworth Beauchamp,
Leicestershire, LE8 0RX
Tel: 0116 279 2299
Email: books@troubador.co.uk
Web: www.troubador.co.uk/matador
Twitter: @matadorbooks

ISBN 978 1789016 765

British Library Cataloguing in Publication Data.
A catalogue record for this book is available from the British Library.

Printed and bound by CPI Group (UK) Ltd, CR0 4YY
Typeset in 12pt Adobe Caslon Pro by Troubador Publishing Ltd, Leicester, UK

Matador is an imprint of Troubador Publishing Ltd

To Carolyn

Contents

I would like to thank all of my friends and family who have helped in putting together these memoirs. In particular, I am grateful to Peter Juggins for his contributions drawn from his deep knowledge of all things Chedworth and his memories of local characters; also for copies of several of the photographs herein. In addition I would like to thank Hazel Barclay and Ruth Henderson for their memories of the village, and my cousin Martin for family background information and for several of his anecdotes regarding our life as children in the village. My thanks to my sister Gail and my wife Carolyn for their suggestions and proofreading. And finally to Pam Morris for her scholarly editing and appraisal of the final manuscript.

Introduction

The west-facing Cotswold escarpment runs, roughly, from Chipping Campden in the north to Bath in the south, and is an area of rolling green hills and honey-grey stone houses and walls. Chedworth lies in a high valley just off the Fosse Way between Cirencester and Northleach and, today, is as picturesque as any Cotswold village. However, the historic reality of these pretty villages was often a life of privation, toil and of necessary self-sufficiency. The Chedworth of my childhood had one foot in the past, with horses still working the land and oil lamps lighting the houses, but was also dipping its other foot into a technological future of cars and electricity. As I grew up, I took the village and its surroundings for granted. It was not until, starting my first job in the late 1950s, getting off the Cirencester bus in a back street of Swindon that I saw a different world. Similarly, five years later when arriving in London to study physics and emerging from the station at Clapham Junction into the smog-shrouded streets of Battersea, I really appreciated the good fortune of having an early life in the Cotswolds. The following pages are based on my memories and, as such, the descriptions of people and places may not be totally accurate.

The numbers in the table refer to the map of Lower Chedworth (opposite) and to the text references

1) *Grove View* – Mrs Holland
2) Mrs Grinnel
3) Amphlett House
3a) Ruin in back garden
4) *Silver Springs* – Mr & Mrs Harvey
5) *Jude Amphlett* – Mr & Mrs Scotford
6) Mr & Mrs Gardner
7) Mr & Mrs McNeil
8) *The Manse* – Mr & Mrs Holland/The Juggins/ The Houghs
9) *The Firs* – Mr & Mrs Petrie
10) The Bridges/Mr & Mrs Jones
11) *Brew House* – Mr Sefton
12) *Hill House* – The Clarks
13) *Gilgal* – Mr & Mrs Hopper
14) Congregational Chapel
15) *Haywards Cottage*
16) *Sweet Briar Cottage*
17) *Box Tree Cottage* – The Goslings
18) *Badger Cottage* – Mr & Mrs Lewis/Mr & Mrs Coleman

19) *Orchard Cottage* – Mr Comley
20) *West Meadow* – Dr & Mrs Watson
21) Ruined cottages
22) *Grey Gables*
23) *Cobblers Cottage* – The Turners
24) *Keens Cottage* – Miss Keen
25) *Bliss Cottage* – The Blisses
26) The Hollands/Mr & Mrs Moier-Williams
27) Farm cottage – The Bulls
28) *Site of Rose Cottage*
29) *York House* – Mr & Mrs Dean
30) *Old Pastures*
31) *Denfurlong House* – Mr & Mrs Keeling/The Bakers
31a) Denfurlong barns
32) Mr & Mrs Millard
33) *Emma's Cottage* – The Carmans
34) Miss Dayment

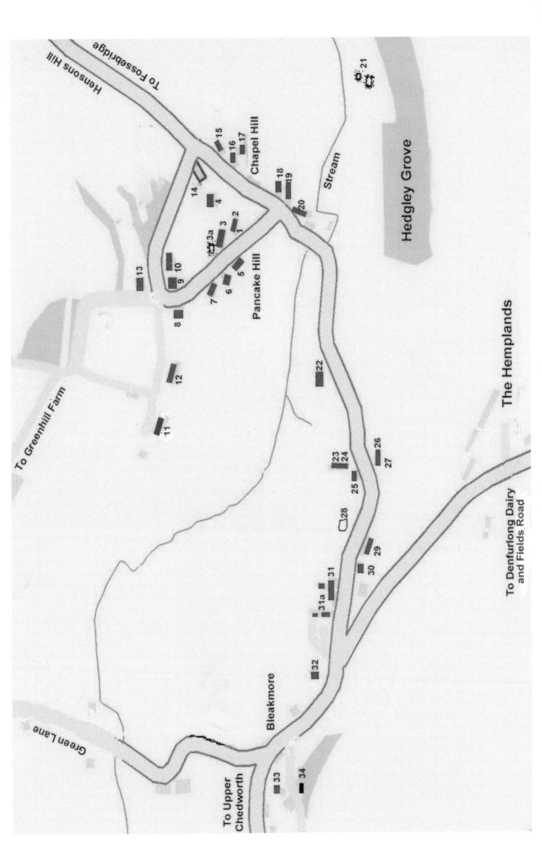

Lower Chedworth

I

The Last Days

The last days of my childhood were also the last days of the village. I belonged to that generation which saw, by chance, the end of a thousand years' life. The change came late to our Cotswold valley, ... but during that handful of years I witnessed the whole thing happen ... Soon the village would break, dissolve, and scatter, become no more than a place for pensioners and wealthy newcomers. It had a few years left, the last of its thousand and they passed almost without our knowing ... The horses had died; few people kept pigs any more but spent their spare time buried in engines.

Laurie Lee – *Cider With Rosie*

Laurie Lee's Slad was not so far in time or place from the Chedworth of my childhood: I also experienced this change in a village, from traditional country life, as it gradually emerged into the 'modern world'; especially after the arrival of electricity, the spread of car ownership and changes in farm practices in the late 1940s and early 1950s. Up until then horses were still widely used, water was drawn from wells and our evenings were lit by oil lamps. I was born in May 1940, on the first day of the Dunkirk evacuation, and spent the first seven years of my life in my grandparents' rambling Cotswold stone house in the lower end of the village. The first five of these were with my mother and grandparents, as during this time my father was posted away in the Army. My brother, Colin, was born when I was two.

The community was close-knit and centred around the church, school and pub. Marriages were often made for company and security – fondness and, possibly, love came later. Agriculture and its supporting services and trades provided the main source of occupation; there was also some employment provided by the railway and the nearby limekiln. Life was hard and the cottages lacked many facilities. Most country people, by necessity, shared a self-reliance which was not specifically taught, but learnt over a lifetime, while tackling the daily tasks that needed to be done. A woman could pluck a chicken, skin a rabbit, salt pork, make jams, pickles and wine, bake pies, cakes and her own bread. She could make rugs, curtains and her own and her children's clothes. A man could do most practical jobs around the house and garden. However, most men had particular skills; for example, my father, being a carpenter, had the skill of sharpening saws which he would do for a small fee, while another neighbour might mend shoes, deal with vermin, mend a roof or even clean out a well.

The village sprawls for about two miles down a narrow, steep-sided valley in a south-easterly direction from the top of the Cotswold Ridge. Over time the valley has been shaped from a gap in the ridge, by melting ice caps, weathering and flowing water. There is a spring line along the side of the valley where oolite, a porous sedimentary limestone, lies on top of an impermeable clay layer. These springs feed a stream which eventually joins the river Coln at Fossebridge.

In the upper end of the village is St. Andrew's Church, the Seven Tuns pub and the manor house. The school is situated about halfway down the village, as was the village hall and railway station. A new village hall has since been built just off Fields Road and the railway station has long since gone.

About a mile north of Upper Chedworth are the historic remains of a Roman villa. Discovered in 1864, it was probably part of a private estate and is one of the largest villas of this type in England.

Chedworth Station

Chedworth station was opened in 1892 on what was then a single track line and was no more than a halt with a 150ft platform. It became double tracked in 1904, but reverted back to a single track in 1929. It had just a booking office and waiting room and was manned by a stationmaster and porters. The main Chedworth station for goods and wartime activities was always Fosse Cross about two miles to the east. It became an unmanned halt in 1956, in the last days by request only, and finally closed in 1961. This sleepy station with embankments decorated with windflowers always reminded me of the poem by Edward Thomas where a steam train makes an unscheduled stop at the north Cotswold station of Adlestrop.

Lower Chedworth, at the other end of the village, lies on the south-facing slope of the valley and forms an inverted triangle with Chapel Hill to the east, Pancake Hill rising to the north-west and the so-called Garbage Lane joining the two at the top (there was an old grassed-over rubbish dump at the chapel end). We lived in Amphlett House which was about halfway up Pancake Hill.

Just north of Lower Chedworth is the picturesque valley of Listercomb with fine views over the river Coln to Stowell Park estate and Stowell Park House. Yanworth, just to the west, is a small rural parish which is part of the Stowell Park estate.

In 1923, Lord Eldon sold the Stowell Park estate to the Vestey family; but before he did so, he sold many of the tied village cottages to his tenants at greatly reduced prices. As a result, it is possible that Chedworth had a higher proportion of owner occupation than other Cotswold villages. This led to a new pride in ownership and opportunities but, through necessity, the upkeep of the houses was often neglected with subsequent structural deterioration.

Upper Paddock

Stowell Park House

Red and white Valerian

Saxifrage

2

Chedworth Cottages

The older cottages in the village were, and remain, picturesque and of typical Cotswold stone construction. Most cottage walls were constructed of variously sized undressed stones with larger squared-off pieces to form the corners and line the doors and windows. Lime mortar was used in the joints and rubble infill used between the inner and outer parts of the wall. Only some of the larger houses, perhaps homes of the wealthy, were constructed of dressed stone. Cotswold limestone varies considerably from one locality to another. Chedworth lies in the mid Cotswolds and here the stone, when first quarried, is a honey-yellow but weathers over time to a soft grey. The character of the cottages was determined by these stones and by the local skills which produced the varied roof lines, window styles, planked doors and ironwork fittings.

The stone of the cottages and surrounding boundary walls hosted a variety of wild flowers. Red and white wild valerian grew out of joints and cracks in the dry stone walls while clumps of succulent saxifrage decorated the tops of field and garden walls.

Without doubt, the most distinctive feature of Cotswold buildings is the use of split stone slates on the roofs which provides a most attractive roofing material. These slates are graduated in size from the bottom to the ridge line. Each slate has a hole drilled in the top and a wooden peg or copper nail is used to fix it to a roof baton. The roof lines are steep and complex, with gables, abundant dormers and prominent chimneys. Stone slates are heavy and substantial timbers are needed to support them. In order to distribute the weight to the walls and to prevent ingress of rainwater, the roofs need a pitch of at least 50 degrees. The original slaters were not only highly skilled, but very inventive. For example, specially cut stones would be used to form weatherproof swept valleys between dormers/gables and the main roof, thus minimising the need for expensive lead-work.

A patchwork of green and golden yellow moss grows across these roofs which, when wet, will sparkle in the sunlight.

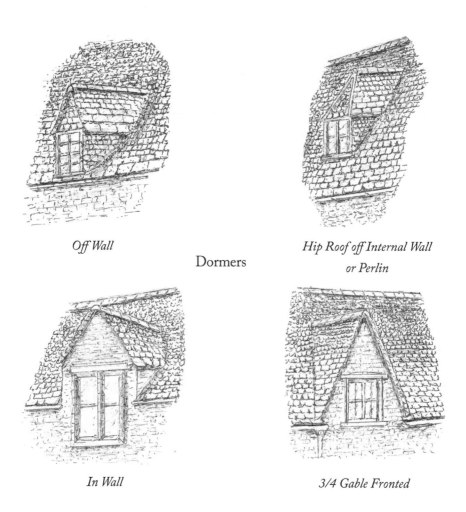

Off Wall

Dormers

Hip Roof off Internal Wall
or Perlin

In Wall

3/4 Gable Fronted

Chimneys were usually built using dressed stone blocks to limit damage from water, and would have a stone cornice and skirt, the latter to protect the chimney/roof joint from ingress of water.

The older windows were often leaded while newer, more decorative windows had bevelled stone surrounds and mullions with hood (drip) moulds above.

Wooden lintel   *Dressed stone arched lintel*   *Drip mould with stone mullion*

The doorways were low with hand-cut planks on the older doors while machine-cut planks came later.

Left – hand-cut plank door with iron ring handle and strap hinges.
Right – newer door with machine-cut planks, internal hinges and thumb lever latch .

Internally, the cottages had low ceilings with exposed beams. The upstairs floors often sloped drunkenly with creaking floorboards, while downstairs the flagstone floors would be covered with oddments of matting. The bigger houses sometimes had inglenook fireplaces, while most cottages had an iron range with a bread oven to the side.

The Cast-Iron Range

Cast-iron ranges were very popular in cottages from the mid-1800s until eventually replaced by gas or electricity. They provided cooking facilities, hot water and heating for the main room. In the centre was the firebox with ash pit underneath. A flue circulated heat around the oven with a damper for temperature regulation. The cast-iron construction meant that the oven held a steady heat for a long time.

Hot water was provided by a tank at the other side or at the back of the range, often with a tap on the front. The trivet at the top of the firebox folded down to form a hob in front of the fire. The top hob over the oven could be very hot and was used for cooking vegetables while the other hob was cooler and used for keeping food and plates warm. A hook or rail attached to the beam above the range could be used to suspend a roast in front of the fire with a drip pan underneath. The chimney breast sometimes contained a separate bread oven, perhaps with its own damper for temperature control.

3

Amphlett House

Amphlett House, where my grandparents lived, was about halfway up Pancake Hill. It had previously been owned by the Broad family and, at one time, George Broad ran a Post Office there. It was probably built in the mid to late eighteenth century and actually consisted of two properties. The original house was two-up, two-down with attics above, cellar below and a wash house/scullery to the side. The adjoining cottage – on the left in the picture opposite – was linked by a door on the ground floor to the main house and was one-up, one-down with attic and wash house. This wash house was referred to as the 'Cats' Bedroom', although there were no cats at that time. The cottage had an old cast-iron range and a spiral staircase, behind a door, to first floor and attic – these spiral staircases are typical of many smaller Cotswold cottages. Steps, at each end of the house, led to a second garden behind – 'the back garden' – which hosted a ruined cottage. There were stables and a carriage/cart house at the end of the property, not used for horses at that time, with a 'tallet' hayloft above, accessed by external stone steps. Water was hand-pumped from a well in the front garden and a lean-to earth closet was hidden at the side of the house behind a lilac tree (see page 29).

The main garden, to the eastern side of the house, was south-facing, with a high stone wall on the northern boundary with a summer house, and along which grew cordon pears, apples and a cherry tree. The back garden was shadier and was used for growing soft fruit, plums and, later, tobacco. There were two paddocks in the valley below the house (see page 4); while I lived at Amphlett House these were rented to Miss Monkton, a lady farmer from Withington. She was eccentric, owned many cats, and came on horseback to inspect her livestock in the paddocks; sitting bolt upright in the saddle she would address my grandparents in a very upper-class accent. Amphlett House was often the focus for family gatherings and early group photographs in my mother's albums show various visiting relatives from both sides of the family. The house is now a Grade II listed building.

Tallet Hayloft

The Tallet is an old West Country name for a loft where hay was kept and then thrown down into the hay racks for the horses below. Outside steps to the feed loft are an essential feature. See page 111.

5 June 1882 – *in his will John Broad left everything to trustees son George Broad (farmer of Amphlett House, Lower Chedworth) and daughter Elizabeth Mary Broad of the same place spinster and to Haines Edward Hooper (Clerk in Holy Orders). Income for his wife until her demise or marriage etc.*

6 November 1884 – *John Broad died.*

3 February 1898 – *Louisa Elizabeth Broad (wife of John) died.*

30 July 1925 – *George Broad rate collector left his estate to sister Elizabeth Mary Broad of Amphlett House.*

20 December 1926 – *George Broad died. EM Broad sole executrix.*

7 December 1927 – *EM Broad made will and appointed cousins EF Cook and C Harvey executors.*

8 October 1928 – *EM Broad died.*

28 January 1929 – *will proved.*

23 March 1929 – *Auction of Freehold Property at Foss Bridge Hotel.*

24 June 1929 – *Ernest Fred Cook of Hill Farm, Chedworth and Cordelia Harvey wife of Thomas Harvey of Silverspring (Vendors and executors of the will of Mary Broad who died 8 Oct 1928) to Frank Louis Foice (retired clerk) of the Highlands, Priory Street, Cheltenham sold Amphlett House with garden and outbuildings thereunto adjoining and the cottage adjoining and belonging to the said dwelling house and all that piece or parcel of land situated near Amphlett House containing 17 perches then in the occupation of William Broad as tenant and two pieces of land with a shed erected numbered 250 and 252 on the OS map for £560.*

Source – Chedworth Society project – *A Survey of Wells in Chedworth*

4

Family Lore

Much of my family background knowledge came from my mother over the years as well as from other family members. However, a significant amount of the background was never discussed with children and a lot of the 'lore' that we gleaned over the years was from overhearing statements and conversations of our elders.

My maternal grandparents came from Wimbledon and were married in 1908. They later moved to New Malden and then to Chedworth in 1929. I know little of my grandfather's background, except that he was born in 1882, with the surname 'Foice' and that he had three brothers and a sister: Fred, Ernest, Harry and Maud. When his father died, his mother, Mary, probably couldn't cope and he was sent to an 'orphan school'. He eventually became an underwriter at Lloyd's of London, but for health reasons was forced to retire early to the sanctuary of the Cotswolds. Because of his early retirement in 1929, my grandparents led a fairly frugal life in Chedworth, but were by no means poor by village standards. My grandfather was certainly intelligent, well read and largely self-taught. He had broad interests and had been something of an athlete, gaining several trophies at fencing. After retirement he learned to read music and play the piano. Although his first name was Frank, my childhood name for him was 'Dadan'.

£sd

Dadan's party trick was to simultaneously add up columns of pounds, shillings and pence in his head. One could give him a list of prices, which he would look at for about ten seconds, before writing the total at the bottom. The normal way of doing this would be to first add up the pence – not forgetting the farthings – divide by twelve and carry forward, writing the remainder under the pence column. Next add up the shillings, divide by twenty, carry forward and write the remainder under the shillings column. Finally add up the pounds. He must have learned this skill during his time at Lloyd's.

Me with Gran Foice

My grandmother, Katie, was born in 1877 and her maiden name was Fielder. She had two brothers: Ernest and William. She could be brusque and quite outspoken. She could not climb the steps up to the back garden and so Dadan would often retreat up there to keep out of the way. One of my earliest memories is of her standing at the bottom of the steps shouting "Frank", to get his attention for meals or to attend to a tradesman. She was also a bit of a snob as, coming from London, she did not consider herself 'country'. Her father George and her brothers had founded a bookshop and photographic studio in Wimbledon. 'Fielders' is still there on Wimbledon Hill Road – now an art and craft shop managed by my second cousin Ian. My grandparents had two daughters: my Aunt Nora and my mother Evelyn.

My mother was born in 1915 and moved to Chedworth with my grandparents at age 14. She then attended Westwood's Grammar School in Northleach for two years, leaving at age sixteen with her General School Certificate. Following this she did a secretarial course at Cheltenham Technical College and gained shorthand and typing qualifications before starting work at Regent Motors in Cheltenham, in an office over the workshops.

Aunt Nora was born in 1909 and remained in London, living with her aunt Maud, after her parents had moved to the Cotswolds. This was because she had quite a good job with a religious magazine. However, although Maud was kind, Nora missed her parents and eventually followed them west. She met my Uncle Reg via my father; Reg lived in Foxcote near Andoversford. He worked in the nearby Kilkeney Inn where his father, William Kilby, was the landlord. Reg and my father became friends and soon they were going out as a foursome with my mother and her older sister, Nora. Nora and Reg were married in 1939 and settled in Cheltenham. They would visit Chedworth several times a year with my cousins, Martin, who was about my age, and Pippa, who was more my sister's age.

My paternal grandparents, Edward and Mabel (née Howlett) had three sons: my father Bob and my uncles Norman and Chris. I saw less of my father's parents who were both in domestic service; he was a valet/butler and she a cook, and so they moved wherever their employment took them.

My father, also born in 1915, was brought up in Foxcote, which is about five miles south-east of Cheltenham. Like my mother he went to Westwood's Grammar School and it was there that they became friends. On leaving school he was apprenticed as a cabinetmaker at Cavendish House, a large department store in Cheltenham. They eventually married in 1938 and lived briefly in Windrush, near Northleach. I was born in 1940. My father volunteered at the outbreak of the Second World War and joined the Royal Engineers. While he was away, my mother moved back to Amphlett

House, now aged 25. I don't think my grandmother had really approved of either of her daughters' choice of marriage partner.

My father's brother, Uncle Norman, had a troubled first marriage before the war, and then spent most of the duration of the war as a guest of the Germans in various prison camps. Soon after his release my mother introduced him to a girl named Daphne. My mother had shared the office at Regent Motors with Daphne and they became lifelong friends – Daphne was my godmother. My mother's motive was partly to help Norman return to a normal life but also to deflect the attention he was giving her while my father was still on the way back from the war in Burma. They married shortly afterwards and settled in Cheltenham, where Norman continued his trade as a plumber.

Uncle Chris served as a boy soldier before the war and during the war, like my father, joined the Royal Engineers. He left the Army in 1948 and shortly afterwards met and married a glamorous Canadian girl, named Phyllis, who worked in the perfume department at a pharmacy in Minehead. They emigrated to Canada in early 1954.

My brother, Colin, was born in 1942; while I was quiet and thoughtful he was quite the opposite, what today would be called hyperactive. Dadan, who had had to retire early after a nervous breakdown, found his mischievous energy difficult to deal with – especially if he found his way into the pantry or workshop. Colin did not seem able to anticipate the consequences of his actions.

A more distant member of the family was Teddy Key who was Dadan's niece Margaret's husband and it was through Margaret that he became a frequent visitor to Amphlett House and shared many interests with Dadan. 'Uncle' Teddy had obtained a double first from Cambridge in history and geography and then for a while was a history master at Cheltenham Grammar School before making a successful application to become head of Dr Morgan's Grammar School in Bridgwater. He was my godfather and was very kind to the family – he always gave me pocket money when visiting, at Christmas and for my birthday.

'I Don't Know' and 'Not Me'

My mother often referred to me as 'I Don't Know' and my younger brother Colin as 'Not Me'. 'Not Me' was quite a mischievous little boy with a restless energy who, according to my mother, was into everything but was, nevertheless, a very lovable and generous boy with an engaging charm and cheerfulness. 'I Don't Know' did his best to shield 'Not Me' and keep him out of trouble. A tablecloth dragged off the table along with the crockery. A cracked window pane. A raided pantry with a telltale trail of sultanas and raisins across the floor. "Who did this?" asked Mother. "Not me," said one; "I don't know," said the other.

There is much evidence of Roman occupation in the countryside surrounding Chedworth, including colonies of the large 'Roman Snails' introduced by them for culinary purposes. My grandfather made field trips with Teddy Key, particularly in the Listercomb area to the north of Lower Chedworth, where they traced concentrations of artefacts such as red clay tile and mosaic fragments. They also found flint fragments in the same area which must have been brought in by early travellers; I still have an arrowhead from their collection of artefacts. Later Uncle Teddy took a party of boys from Cheltenham Grammar School to conduct

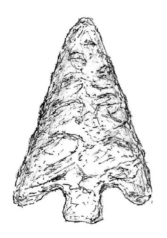

an excavation at the Listercomb Roman site. However, they found that all of the buildings had been robbed or quarried for stone and the small amount of pavement that was uncovered was apparently re-buried as being of too little significance compared with that at the existing Roman Villa in the next valley which had been discovered in 1864 and excavated by Lord Eldon.

Dadan with 'Uncle' Pat

Although not 'family', another frequent visitor to Amphlett House was 'Uncle' Pat. He was an old family friend of my grandparents from Wimbledon and would visit Amphlett House several times a year. Dadan always enjoyed the visits of his old friend – if only for the walk down the valley to the Fossebridge Hotel for a pint.

There were other family members, not so close, who were nevertheless regular visitors to Amphlett House. There was Dadan's brother Fred (who had 'Foices' hairdressing business in Cheltenham), Fred's son Eric and wife Sylvia, and their son Michael. It was Fred who supported Dadan after leaving London and helped him to find sanctuary in the Cotswolds. They came across Amphlett House, which was for sale, during one of their weekend hikes. On my grandmother's side there was her brother William ('Uncle' Willie), William's son Norman (who had a glass eye) and his wife Betty with their children Ian and Gillian – who both became childhood friends of mine. As mentioned earlier, Ian now manages the family business in Wimbledon. What with visitors, and my mother and two boys during the war years, Dadan did not always get the sanctuary he was seeking.

5

Our Neighbours

Chedworth is a sprawling village stretching for over two miles from Lower Chedworth just above Fossebridge and the river Coln up to The Laines high on the watershed of the Cotswold ridge. Lower Chedworth is in effect a separate hamlet, dependent, however, on the amenities of Middle and Upper Chedworth. With the wind in the east, the sound of the bells from the Church of St. James the Great in Coln St. Dennis, near Fossebridge, would come up the valley, fading and soaring with the wind. However, if the wind was down the valley, it would be the bells from St. Andrew's Church at the top of the village that would reach our ears.

Because of the spread of the village we were most familiar with those close by, although we probably knew the name and business of most people in the wider village. Our immediate neighbour was Mrs Holland who lived just below us in Grove View (1). She was a cheerful lady who owned a small spaniel and would often invite us children into her cottage and offer us a glass of lemonade. The cottage had a damp, musty smell and the sideboard and shelves were covered in floral Victorian china. There was a deep well in her outhouse with a cast-iron pump on top. She owned the adjoining cottage (2) which she let to Mrs Grinnel who was said to be a bit gloomy and awkward – although, as children, we got on with her well enough. She did housework for my grandparents and when my grandmother wanted to communicate with her she would take a stone, which she kept for the purpose, and knock it on the back wall of Mrs Grinnel's cottage; they could then converse across the garden wall.

The Shooting of Bill Gardner

Bill Gardner was shot, near his home, by another postman named Frederick Broad on the morning of 23 December 1924. As a result his lower jaw was almost shot away and he also suffered severe shotgun wounds to his right thigh and hand. The motive is unclear, but was probably a dispute over promotion and the allocation of postal rounds, although some say that it was something to do with a young lady. Frederick Broad, thinking he had killed Bill Gardner, left the scene and was witnessed walking along Horses Ash Lane in the direction of Chedworth Woods. There he took his own life by throwing himself in front of an early morning passenger train near the north portal of Chedworth tunnel. His dismembered body was found later in the day by a railway ganger. Bill Gardner was taken to Cirencester Memorial Hospital where it was felt that there was little hope of his recovery. However, he did recover and worked on as a postman for many years. Needless to say, this tragic event, in a quiet country village, shocked the entire community.

John Scotford and his wife lived opposite us on Pancake Hill (5). John was a kindly old man who kept bees. He and Dadan got on well and spent a lot of time chatting about gardening and other matters. As well as being a source of excellent honey, his wife would occasionally present us with jars of her home made jams and pickles. Bill Gardner and his wife lived up the hill (6), next door to the Scotfords. Bill was our postman at the time, who because of a village feud had most of his lower jaw missing. As a result, he had a severe speech impediment and dribbled continually. He also had a bad limp. The story of the village feud which led to his injury is well documented elsewhere (and see box above); suffice to say, my mother told me that he had been shot by another postman in a personal dispute, and not to stare. Further up the hill (7), lived Mary Broad with her daughter – also named Mary. They took a lodger named Arthur (Jock) McNeil. He worked in Cirencester and was one of the few car owners in Lower Chedworth. Young Mary fell in love with Jock and they got married soon after the death of Mary Broad senior.

At the top of Pancake Hill, on the left, was the Manse (8), which was owned by the Congregational Chapel. Before the war it was occupied by Rev. Watkins and after that, during the war, by Mr Stentiford. It was Mr Stentiford who started having the band at the chapel for the annual Harvest Festival. After the war, the Manse was briefly rented by the Dales with their son Martin who, while he lived there, was a good friend of mine. Then, for several years, it was rented by Geoff and Joyce Holland. The Manse became a private dwelling in 1955 when it was bought from the church by Bert and May Juggins. They had five children but at that time only one (Monica) lived there with them. Peter, the second son, was a builder and stonemason who became well known locally for the outstanding work he did in the restoration of local buildings and churches. The Manse was eventually bought by Richard Hough, the author and historian. He specialised in maritime history and biographies and wrote a definitive biography of Lord Mountbatten, *Hero of our Time*.

Peter Juggins

Peter Juggins was born in 1927 and spent most of his life in Chedworth. He is one of the few people today who has a deep knowledge of all things 'Chedworth'. He went to the village school and left at the age of fourteen to do building work for Mustoes in Northleach. During the war he was employed on essential building work, including the new airfield and on Stowell Park hospital. He joined Chedworth silver band at the age of eleven and played in military bands during his national service. Afterwards, while he was working for a Cirencester building firm, the stonemason had a stroke and Peter was asked to carry on under the stonemason's instruction – and so Peter learnt his skills with stone. Over the years he has worked on many stone-masonry projects including: Bishop's Cleeve church windows, forty-three pinnacles and gargoyles for Fairford church and the south wall windows of St. Andrew's Church in Chedworth. He married Gloria Richards in 1953, was a long-term parish councillor and is an accomplished artist.

A track on the left, at the top of Pancake Hill, leads to Hill House (12) owned by Cliff and Mary Clark. They had two daughters – Joanne and Elizabeth – and they were all good family friends of ours. They kept a smallholding with ducks, chickens and pigs. Cliff Clark owned a vintage Lagonda and we would often accompany them to old car events such as rallies and hill climbs. Cliff Clark was something of a mentor to me and I would frequently help him with the animals or work on his old cars.

Beyond Hill House was Brew House (11); Mr Sefton lived there and during and after the war he was seconded by the War Office and put in charge of ration coupons and other administrative matters for the area. He used to walk the five miles, every day, to his office in Northleach. His daughter lived in a small cottage attached to Brew House.

Also at the top of Pancake Hill, on the right, was a cottage called The Firs (9). Daisy Broad, who was a widow, lived there and eventually married Donald Petrie who was her 'lodger'. Mr Petrie worked for the council as road-man maintaining the roadsides in the village. In summer he cut and trimmed the verges and in autumn cleared the ditches of leaves and other debris deposited by the wind and rain. He was a garrulous man and would need no encouragement to stop his work at the roadside and pass the time of day, often delaying our return from school with his stories. He also cut people's hair in the village (with scissors and clippers, not his sickle!) and would visit Amphlett House when my brother and I needed a good trim.

Harry and Betty Bridges with their two sons, Graham and Ricky, lived in a bungalow on Garbage Lane (10). Harry Bridges owned a small building firm as had his father, also named Harry. Graham and Ricky, who owned two ponies, were our main childhood friends in the village. Graham rode in gymkhanas and also got me on to the back of a horse for the first and only time in my life. Harry eventually built a new house for the family on the Fosse Way at the top of Fossebridge Hill. They sold the bungalow to Alec and Freda Jones. Freda was a concert pianist and taught the piano to local children, including my sister, Gail.

Tom and Annie Gosling lived in Box Tree Cottage halfway down Chapel Hill (17). They had three daughters – Merle, Hazel and Shirley. They were cousins to the Juggins children and all childhood friends of ours.

At the bottom of Pancake Hill, on the opposite side of the road, was Badger Cottage (18). From the 1850s it had been occupied by the Colletts who were a family of boot and shoemakers, and general leather workers (harnesses, saddles etc.). Later the cottage was occupied by Robin and Doreen Lewis and in the 1950s by Mr and Mrs Coleman. Mrs Coleman wrote children's books and took an interest in the education of some of the local children. She tutored me and Hazel Gosling in writing and arithmetic prior to taking the eleven-plus. I remember there was a large inglenook fireplace with seats built in on each side.

Next to Badger Cottage was a cottage now named Orchard Cottage (19). This was occupied by a Mr Comley. He had poor eyesight and was a bit of a hermit, although he got on well enough with Dadan. There must have been a problem with his chimney as he would come to his door blinking and surrounded by wood smoke.

The Collett family outside Badger Cottage

At the bottom of Chapel Hill was West Meadow (20) occupied by Dr & Mrs Watson. They kept goats in their paddock and showed me how to milk them and then filter the milk ready for cooling.

Although there were other villagers living nearby, these are the characters that I remember most. Lower Chedworth was, then, a small community somewhat remote from the rest of the village and, without cars, we were largely dependent on a bus service which terminated at the bottom of Pancake Hill.

West Meadow

6

Life at Amphlett House

Many houses in the village had wells, equipped with either a windlass or a small cast-iron pump. Amphlett House was a bit more 'modern' – it had a tall, long-handled pump which was connected directly to a storage tank in the attic. The hot water was provided by a back boiler on an anthracite stove in the dining room. The hot water tank was in a partitioned-off area of the attic which also contained a washbasin and bath.

A paraffin-fired range had been installed in the scullery which also housed a large rainwater tank and a glazed earthenware sink with hot, cold and rainwater taps. Waste water seemed to discharge under flagstones in the side yard – there may have been a soakaway somewhere. There was a 'copper' (a large boiler) in the corner which was no longer in use, but prior to the installation of the range would have been used for laundry and to provide hot water for baths. The water in the copper was heated by a coal fire which was lit through an opening in the supporting brickwork.

The wooden seat on the earth closet at the side of the house was furnished with two holes; one was standard size and the other a smaller hole for younger members of the family. A shaker of Jeyes Powder was provided to keep smells and flies at bay, and occasionally dry earth would be sprinkled in. Once a year Dadan would dig a bean trench the length of the garden. He would then light his pipe, take a couple of strong puffs, raise the closet seat and using a long-handled shovel he would dig out the contents and barrow it to the bean trench. Surprisingly, the product, after treatment with dry earth, looked like garden compost and had very little smell – the beans certainly grew well and were probably very tasty. My mother did not think that these outside facilities were suitable for two young children and, as my brother Colin and I approached school age, Dadan installed a chemical toilet in the cottage scullery ('Cats' Bedroom').

Our evenings were lit by oil lamps and candles.

Paraffin oil lamps hung from the ceilings of the main rooms and cast a rather dim yellow light. However, Dadan had an Aladdin lamp on the table

beside his armchair. The Aladdin lamp has a gauze mantle which glows with a brilliant white light. The mantle, which is made of a special mixture of rare earth oxides, is far more efficient than a simple lamp wick.

Candles were used at bedtime and, while climbing the stairs up to the attic bedroom, the flickering candle flame would cast dancing shadow monsters onto the whitewashed ceilings.

In winter the attic bedrooms were very cold and I would wake up peering from underneath my eiderdown at frost patterns on the inside of the windows. All of the bedrooms were equipped with chamber pots, as going outside with no light and, of course, no heating was not really an option. Downstairs, in the evenings, the draught would blow in through the ill-fitting plank doors from one end of the house to the other. In the living room, which had a board floor over the cellar, the lino would lift and fall as air blew in through an air brick below.

The radios used batteries – a high-voltage dry cell and a low-voltage accumulator to power the valve filaments. Two sets of accumulators were required – one set in use and the other set having their weekly charge at Currys, necessitating regular bus trips to Cirencester.

Dadan's morning routine was to do the chores – pump the water, fill the coal scuttles, trim the wicks of the lamps and top them up with paraffin. That done he would have his elevenses: coffee, a biscuit and a glass of Keystone British Burgundy. I don't know whether he believed that 'ferruginous' indicated that it was good for the blood, but I think he drank it because, in those days, it was far cheaper than imported wine. In the meantime, if the weather was fair, my grandmother would take a colander up to the summer house and prepare vegetables for dinner – which was always taken at 12.30.

My preschool days were spent mostly with my grandfather in his workshop – where he made us many wooden toys – or, when it was fine, out in the garden. He had an extensive library, including the works of Shakespeare, Dickens and several poets, plus books on botany, anatomy, philosophy and history. He had a number of science volumes: for example, *Science for the Citizen* and *Mathematics for the Million* by Lancelot Hogben who did a lot to popularise science in the 1930s; also several volumes on astronomy by Sir James Jeans who was the Patrick Moore of the day. I still have many of his books.

Before I was five I knew the names of the planets and, with my grandfather, would listen to the Home Service to programmes on topics such as Hubble's latest theories on the universe. I remember him, on one occasion, trying to explain to me the difference between a galaxy and a nebula, though I am not sure that he was quite clear on this himself.

All too soon the idyll was over and it was time for me to start school. It was Merle Gosling, who was two or three years older than me, who was tasked with escorting a pale-faced and very quiet boy up to the village school. Like most, I had to make a big adjustment with new surroundings, different routines and the sheer number of often boisterous children.

The Tragic Death of Merle Gosling

On leaving school, Merle became a nurse at Northleach Hospital. On 21 August 1958, aged twenty-one, she was returning home in hospital transport. As the vehicle left Northleach and was moving up the hill on the Fosse Way from the junction with the A40, a door somehow flew open and Merle was thrown out onto the road. She received severe injuries from which she died three days later. I had left school and was working near Swindon at the time. I was shocked and upset when I heard of this tragic accident.

Gran Foice with me in a pushchair at Amphlett House in the early 1940s

Common Vetch

7

Village Services and Supplies

With only an infrequent bus service and before widespread ownership of cars, we depended on our doorstep services, which also provided a lot of the local news and gossip, and relief from the isolation and tedium of everyday routine.

A horse-drawn cart brought milk, in churns, directly from Denfurlong (Finch's) dairy on the south side of the valley. We would take our milk jugs to the cart where Horace Jelf, the milkman, would use pint or half-pint dippers to measure the milk into the jugs. In summer the milk had to be heated immediately to boiling point; this preserved it for twenty-four hours, but gave it a strange taste. Horace was married to Mabel (nee Akers) who was brought up on Woodlands Farm at Pinswal, near the top of the village, where her parents were employed by the Finches. Horace wore a long brown smock and both he and his

Horace

cart had a strong smell of sour milk. He was a jovial character and a great tease, and when he came to the house for his weekly money he would lift my baby brother from the playpen under the dining room window and, winking at me, would threaten to take him away.

Bread was delivered in a canvas-covered wagon from the village bakery which was located behind the village shop. The baker came to the door with a large wicker basket of loaves – mostly we took the large quartern loaves with crisp, knobbly crusts on top. When he was younger Peter Juggins worked on Saturdays for Walker's bakery, delivering bread with Mr Walker from a horse and cart, in Chedworth and to the villages down the Coln Valley. He well remembers delivering to my grandparents, as Dadan had a digestive problem and Walkers baked a very hard wholegrain loaf for him every week.

The unfortunate Bill Gardner who lived near us on Pancake Hill (6) was our postman and, as mentioned earlier, had most of his lower jaw missing as a result of a village feud. Our coal was delivered by Reg Harvey, at first by horse and wagon – the coat of the horse was black with coal dust as was Reg's face and clothing. A lorry was later used for coal delivery.

The policeman after the war was PC Ron Hill; most of the time there was not much action needing his attention and he would push his bicycle round the village and chat to people he met on his way. The police station was at the bottom of Well Hill, below the school, and had a cell, then unused, with barred windows; I think it had mostly been used in the past for sobering up drunks overnight.

The local blacksmith, Mr Crump, had a forge near Fossebridge and we would often watch him shoeing carthorses or working at the forge and anvil, repairing farm machinery.

Often I would accompany my grandmother on her weekly visit to nearby Greenhill (Dunstan's) Farm to collect eggs. As she chatted in the farmhouse kitchen with Edith Dunstan I would explore the farmyard and try to make friends with the barn cats. Edith's brothers, Jim and Don, ran the farm and if they were working in the farmyard I had them for company. The farmhouse kitchen was the heart of the farm with a large range and a big, deeply grooved, deal table. What fascinated me was the copperware on a large dresser and hung from the walls. In particular I was intrigued by an elaborate copper samovar on a shelf, its polished complexity reflecting light from a nearby window.

Walker's shop supplied our day-to-day needs. Dry goods were weighed out from large sacks which stood around the worn flagstone floor. There was no refrigeration and the more perishable goods were often not as fresh as they should be. The cheese, known as 'mouse trap', would be hard and cracked. Butter was often rancid and I can remember my embarrassment when my mother sent me back to the shop with it to demand a refund.

Beyond the basic goods available in the village shop it was necessary to get the local bus to Cirencester or Cheltenham. Harvey's Coaches was based in Chedworth and operated several Bedford buses. During and immediately after the war these were utility vehicles which had wooden seats and very little internal trim. My grandmother always complained bitterly about the discomfort of these seats, especially when the bus was negotiating some of the rougher country roads.

Harvey's Bedford OB. Outside the Old Packhorse Inn at Ampney St. Peter –
by David Christie.

Later, they ran Bedford OBs. The gearbox in this Bedford had a very characteristic whine and, returning from Cheltenham, the bus would grind slowly up Dowdeswell Hill and then up Withington Hill to The Laines and the old airfield at the top of Chedworth. At almost 830ft this is one of the highest points on the Cotswold ridge. In winter the windows, closed against the cold, would steam up and trap a fug of cheap perfume, sweat and cigarette smoke. In summer the bus would sometimes pull carefully past a horse and cart with a local farmer from Withington fast asleep in the back alongside a crate of beer. He would be returning from an afternoon in the Royal Well Tavern. His horse knew the way back to the farm and on arrival would wait patiently in the yard for his master to wake up.

Harvey's Buses

In the early 1900s Jack Laurence bought a charabanc with the idea that he could take people to the shops in Cheltenham at more convenient times than the train and deliver them to the centre of town. However, the vehicle was unreliable and kept breaking down. Frank Harvey, a haulier, and his son Ralph bought the charabanc and at one time it was even used to take sheep to the livestock market in Cirencester. In the end Frank and Ralph acquired three buses and, as well as the school run, set up regular services to Cirencester and Cheltenham. During the war they ran utility Bedfords; these were called threepenny bits (after the old brass, twelve-sided coin), because all the steel presses had been commandeered for military vehicle production and the bus panels had to be creased and bent into shape. Fred Miles and Harold Andrews were the bus drivers at the time. The Bedford OBs, which Harvey's used after the war, were not always popular with the drivers and Harold Andrews, who could be a bit irascible, was sometimes heard to mutter, "Bedfords is tripe."

8

The War Years

Rationing started in January 1940 for many foodstuffs and was followed by clothing rationing in June 1941. However, in some ways, this had a limited impact on the village because people grew their own vegetables, kept chickens and were prepared to trade coupons for things they did need. Powdered eggs, which had a bright yellow colour and came in waxed brown cartons, were regarded with disdain – only good for baking. Woolton pies, an adaptable inexpensive dish of vegetables devised by Lord Woolton, head of the Ministry of Food at the time, were also available weekly at the village hall, but there was very little take-up.

Wire or concrete tank traps were prepared at strategic points on the local roads. There was also some evidence of Home Guard activity – such as brushwood shelters in the woods.

As with many villages across the south of England, an airfield was built near Chedworth, on level land at the top of the village. It was completed in 1942 and used throughout the war by the RAF for training in various aircraft. It acted as a satellite airfield, mainly to Aston Down to the south-east of Stroud. At the peak of operations there were around 600 personnel and crew, housed mostly around the airfield in purpose-built accommodation. It was said to be unpopular with pilots due to unpredictable crosswinds – at the time it was the highest airfield in the UK. After the war it was used as a depot to store hundreds of surplus military vehicles and containers of equipment.

During the 1950s the runways were used for motor racing events and by gliding clubs. They were also used extensively by learner drivers – including my mother and later myself. One of the disused buildings was converted into our scout headquarters and we camped there on several occasions.

Another major installation at the time was the 160th US General Hospital which was housed in Nissen huts within the grounds of Stowell Park House (page 5) between Fossebridge and Northleach. It was opened in December 1943 to cater for anticipated war casualties. Up to and following D-Day, the wounded were brought, via ambulance train, to nearby Fosse Cross station. Apparently pioneering heart surgery procedures were developed here – in particular the removal of shrapnel from a beating heart. There was also a neurosurgery department.

The American servicemen soon made friends within the village and two male nurses became particular friends with my family, spending a lot of their off-duty time at Amphlett House. These were big fellows, over six feet tall, and they would toss me around on the front lawn as if I was a ball. My mother told me later that some of the patients at the hospital were shell-shocked and violent; strong nurses were required for their own safety and the safety of others. Although wartime rationing had a limited impact in a country village, the occasional offerings from our American friends were very welcome. I particularly remember Hershey's chocolate and the tubes of Life Savers – hollow sweets, similar to Polo mints, but in different flavours, including the rather curious green Wint-o-Green. After the war the Stowell Park camp was used as a Polish resettlement centre and school. My family kept in touch with their American friends for many years after the war, and I was even able to stay with one family, near Niagara Falls, during a postgraduate working vacation.

The railway line through Chedworth was part of the Midland and South Western Junction Railway (M&SWJR), which formed a link from the Midlands to the port of Southampton. The section through Chedworth ran from Cheltenham Lansdown, via Cirencester to Swindon Old Town. It was opened in 1891 and closed in 1961. It became especially important in the build-up to the invasion of Normandy in 1944 and I remember standing on the bridge where Fields Road (or the Top Road as we knew it at the time) crossed the line and watching heavy goods trains pass through, many with tanks on flatbed wagons.

I think Dadan was some sort of warden at the time. There was a substantial stockpile of medical supplies in a cupboard in his workshop and he was issued with stirrup pumps and fire buckets. One day in the spring of 1942, an escaping German bomber, returning from a raid on Midland industrial areas, dropped its unreleased cargo of bombs in the fields of Listercomb Bottom in an attempt to evade British fighters and get home quickly. It was Dadan's job to measure the size and distribution of the craters and file his report.

My own memories of the time are very sketchy. I seem to remember Dadan taking me up to the top of the village to watch fighter aircraft crossing from the airfield. I also remember him taking me up to Greenhill Farm (Dunstan's) to watch Italian prisoners of war working in the fields. They seemed fairly content, chatting among themselves – they must have considered themselves lucky to be out of it; anyway, there seemed to be no sign of guards. Many of the Italians stayed on after the war, especially in the Swindon area. I also recall sitting on the front wall next to the sundial at Amphlett House and passing neighbours asking me, "Where's your daddy now?" I was not sure I knew the man they were referring to, but I had certainly been told by my mother to reply, "My daddy's in Burma."

One day, probably during 1944, my mother took Colin and me for a short break with her in-laws. At the time they were living in Tewkesbury in a small tied cottage on the High Street, which runs steeply downhill to a bridge over the river Avon. My brother was put to bed in a drawer taken from a chest of drawers and I was put into a small, rather grubby-looking bed in the corner of the same room. The street is on the main A38 trunk road and was used as part of the route from Liverpool docks to the south coast during the preparations for D-Day. I can remember sitting on a concrete tank trap at the bridge and chatting to the bridge marshal as, day and night, seemingly endless convoys of military vehicles made their way south in preparation for D-Day. The American soldiers waved cheerfully as they went past. It was during this stay that I woke up in the night screaming – I was covered in flea bites. My mother rushed into the room and, soothing me, swore never to return to this filthy house.

My mother was a reasonable piano player and with Harry Bridges on saxophone, plus a drummer, re-formed the small band Harry had had during the 1930s. He was a builder who, because of his trade, was involved in work on military installations and was exempt from active service. The Bridges were relatively well off, possibly because there was money to be made in urgent wartime construction. The band would play in local halls, including at the American bases. In later years my mother confessed coyly to me that she had been 'a naughty girl' at the time. But this was not unusual during the war when so many men, including my father, were posted overseas for a very long time. After the war my father became the band drummer. Mrs Grinnel, who was a neighbour of my grandparents, would babysit us on Saturday nights while our parents were out playing in the band.

For the VE Day fete, Dadan made several amusements. I remember one in particular which involved a pinball-type chute down which one had to guide a golf ball and try to get it through the door of a palace. If successful, flags would fly up from the roof. We played with this for years after the event. Several children, including me, were drilled for some days beforehand at dancing round the maypole. Eventually, we could wind up the ribbons into a neat plait and unwind them without creating a tangled mess. Chedworth silver band entertained and as usual there was bowling for the pig; this was played with large wooden skittles in an enclosure of stacked-up straw bales using the only flat piece of grass available, the pig being delivered to the winner at a later date. The children were organised into fun games such as three-legged and sack races. Some of the games, such as British Bulldog, were not so gentle. When leaving, the children were presented with a certificate and commemorative mug.

9

The Soldiers' Return

For many returning soldiers, life for them and their families would never be the same as before the war. On returning to civilian life they found it difficult to settle, with limited opportunities, and some will have suffered from physical and mental problems. Their families would have moved on and considerable readjustment was required, especially for the young.

The war in Europe ended on 8 May 1945. However, for my father and the troops involved in the Burma campaign – the 'Forgotten War' – hostilities did not end until August of that year with the capitulation of Japan and then there was the long journey home by troop ship.

In Melvyn Bragg's book *The Soldier's Return*, Sam Richardson returns in 1946 from Burma. The discipline of service life and the campaign in Burma have changed him. Back in civilian life he feels restricted and restless. At home his wife Ellen and his six-year-old son Joe have lived a sheltered life, in a large house, with Ellen's aunt and uncle. Joe barely remembers his father and all three struggle to adjust. Ellen and Sam find it difficult to talk about the things that matter most to them. Sam feels that his son has been sheltered and is not as rough and tough as he should be, while Joe is not at ease with his father and half fears him. For Joe his best days were before his father came back and he frequently seeks sanctuary in the old house with his great-aunt and uncle.

My grandfather was an attentive and gentle man and my grandmother indulgent with us boys and so my father's return from Burma late in 1945 came as a shock. He was a stranger – I had perhaps met him once or twice when he came home on leave, before he was sent overseas. My brother and I were normal children: often boisterous, sometimes mischievous, especially my brother. My father did not find it easy to relate to us, he did not have a lot of conversation to offer and almost never played games with us. In response to our behaviour he fell back on discipline and as we grew older his patience became shorter and the discipline more severe. Corporal punishment was not unusual in those days in a country village; at primary school the older boys were regularly caned hard across the hands and home life stories, during playground chatter, revealed similar parental discipline.

Like Melvyn Bragg's Sam, my father spoke little of his time in Burma, though unlike Sam, he had seen no front-line action and encountered very few Japanese. He was in the Royal Engineers, involved with building roads and bridges in preparation for the logistics of front-line reinforcement. He certainly spoke highly of the Bailey bridge, saying that it was a good, simple design. He said it needed no special transport and that he could supervise erection of a bridge by a platoon of forty men in three hours. The bridge could then carry the weight of the heaviest tanks.

Unlike Sam, my father did not find the return to home life empty and meaningless; he immediately applied himself to first planning and then building a house (Grey Gables) into which we moved in 1947 (See 22 on map). Thereafter, like Joe, I often sought sanctuary with my grandparents back in the old house, in order to avoid my father's moods.

Early on in the war my Uncle Norman was captured by the Germans just outside of Dunkirk. He spent the rest of the war in prison camps where their diet was poor, particularly towards the end when they were marched eastwards between camps, and had to rely a lot on what they could scavenge from the fields. On release, they were counselled by dieticians who advised a graduated return to normal eating. He ignored all advice and indulged immediately in rich foods – fish and chips, pies etc. As a result he suffered from stomach ulcers and other digestive problems for the rest of his life.

In 1942 my Uncle Chris was posted as part of the 8th Army in the Desert Campaign. He then became part of Wingate's Chindits phantom army operating behind the Japanese lines in Burma. After this jungle adventure he spent several months in rehabilitation in India, following which he was posted back to England where he was assigned to bomb disposal. He left the Army in 1948 but, like many ex-servicemen, could not settle and was unable to find decent work. After he married, he and his Canadian wife, Phyllis, lived in Cheltenham for a while but I am sure she soon persuaded him that their prospects in Canada would be much better. They left for Canada, with their son (my cousin Lee), in 1954 on board the *Empress of France*.

The Burma Campaign
The Role of the Chindits and Sappers

The initial campaigns of 1942–43, led by Lieutenant-General Slim, were difficult with the British being repeatedly driven back by the Japanese. The more orthodox tactics of the British commanders were no match for the Japanese who could win with smaller, more flexible and mobile units in the dense Burmese jungle. At the time, Burma was an isolated country with no more than tracks connecting it to India. On the western borders of northern Burma were mountainous jungle ranges, impenetrable bamboo forests and tortuous rain-drenched river valleys.

Early 1944 saw the start of a major offensive by the Allies. Its success was almost certainly made possible, in no small part, by the unorthodox tactics of Major-General Wingate's Chindits who adopted guerrilla tactics deep behind enemy lines. The Chindits were made up of mainly British and Gurkha jungle-trained regulars – the name Chindit was derived from the mythical beasts whose statues guarded most of the Burmese temples. More unconventional were the Special Operations Executive (SOE) who operated behind enemy lines with local guerrillas – the latter not always trusted as their aim was to get rid of, first, the Japanese, and then the British. All of these behind-the-lines activities depended heavily on air drops made in total darkness over unmapped territory.

By 8 January, Akyab Island off the west coast was back in British hands – this was important for its deep-water port and all-weather airfield. The push into the testing terrain of Arkan on the western mainland began. Vast engineering effort was required to build all the infrastructure necessary to support the advancing armies, including roads, bridges, airstrips to enable Dakotas to land equipment and evacuate casualties, depots for ammunition and fuel, and even huge stock farms. On the British front this was all coordinated by the Royal Engineers (Sappers) supported by tens of thousands of Indian labourers. The work of the Royal Engineers and the activities of the Chindits on both sides of the lines continued throughout the campaign until victory in Burma in August 1945.

10

Events of 1947

The winter of 1946–47 was severe with low temperatures and prolonged snowfall. Heavy snow fell from 21 January and the roads soon became impassable. The thaw did not start until mid March. It was said to be the worst for snowfall since the winter of 1913–14. Hundreds of villages were cut off by deep drifts, including Chedworth. Strong easterly winds blew, creating mountainous drifts across the main A429 – the Fosse Way – and across the roads at the top of the village. Local effort to clear the Fosse Way through to Cirencester was slow and the eventual breakthrough was only achieved with the help of military tractors (Antars) which had been left by the Americans at Stowell Park. Work on Grey Gables came to a halt for several weeks and the roofless house lay under snow-covered tarpaulins. I remember playing in the garden of Amphlett House among snow drifts higher than my six years and walking, with my father, the one and a half miles back from the station to the old house in a near-blizzard. I walked behind him for shelter and tried to pick up his footsteps – like Good King Wenceslas and page. I think we were returning from Cheltenham after visiting my mother, who was in a nursing home, following the arrival of my sister.

My sister Gail was born that January and for me this was the second major event of that year. Being seven years older than her I always felt very protective towards her. I remember pushing her in her pram along the road from Grey Gables.

Gail

The move from the old house to Grey Gables (see 22 on map) took place in the summer of 1947 – not that there was much to move. The house was largely undecorated, the floors bare and the garden still a building site. For the first month or two we relied on bottled gas and oil lamps, although we now had a flush toilet. All of my father's service pay had been ploughed into the new house and so for several years we lived in relative poverty – there was little meat at that time and we were grateful when the odd rabbit was dumped on the doorstep by a kindly neighbour. My father, having been apprenticed as a cabinetmaker, made a lot of our furniture. My mother clothed us as best she could and made rag rugs from offcuts and old clothes by looping small rectangles of material through a hessian backing.

Our water now came, not from a well, but from a spring which surfaced about half a mile down the valley towards Fossebridge where a hydraulic ram was used to pump water up to a storage tank on a mound above the quarry adjacent to Denfurlong (Finch's) dairy. I think it was set up by Cecil Finch to supply water to the farm buildings and surrounding cottages. The Finches had owned Woodlands Farm since 1928 and purchased Denfurlong Farm in 1938 for use as a dairy.

The Hydraulic Ram

A hydraulic ram uses no external power and so is very useful in remote areas where there is no electricity. It uses the momentum of a large amount of water, falling a few feet, to pump a relatively small amount of water uphill to the storage tank, which could be 100 feet or more above the source. It is very simple and utilises the water hammer effect of a surge entering a chamber. A spring-loaded waste 'clack' valve would be forced shut giving water from the chamber enough pressure to open a delivery 'check' valve.

The final big event of 1947 was the arrival of electricity in Lower Chedworth. Tree fellers preceded the pole erection and cable rigging. I don't think they had much idea of the cable routes and seemed to cut down trees at random. For years the trunks lay rotting on the ground nowhere near the power lines. Hot on the heels of the electricity engineers came the domestic appliance salesmen trying to sell to sceptical country folk who, they thought, might be gullible. I remember my grandmother fixing a young vacuum cleaner salesman with a sceptical look. "Young man," she exclaimed, "we have managed all our lives without these gadgets; we will carry on beating the carpets over the washing line."

The Bridges, who were relatively well off, were one of the first in our locality to own a refrigerator; I well remember that Betty Bridges used to make a type of custard ice cream in the freezer compartment. They were also probably one of the first families in the village to own a television.

It was soon after electricity came to the village that Dadan, with the help of Uncle Pat's engineering expertise, installed an electric pump to the well at Amphlett House; so ended the daily chore of hand-pumping the water.

II

New Neighbours

After we moved to Grey Gables our nearest neighbours were now up the road towards the middle of the village. On the other side of our paddock there was a pair of cottages; the one nearest the road, now named Keens Cottage (24 on map), was purchased by William Keen when Lord Eldon sold the Stowell Park estate in 1923. When William died the cottage was inherited by his daughter, Patience. At the bottom of her garden, nearest to our house, there was a well with a cast-iron pump. Because of the leather valves, these old pumps often needed priming with a small amount of water kept back from the previous session. My brother and I shared a bedroom overlooking Patience's garden and would be woken by the sound of a slosh of water followed by the *creak-clank, creak-clank* of the pump – we then knew that it was time to get out of bed and get ready for school. In any case, Mother would soon be shouting, "Boys, get up!" from the bottom of the stairs.

The adjoining cottage, Cobblers Cottage (23), used to be owned by one of the Collet family who were involved in the cobblers' trade; he was a shoemaker in the early twentieth century. Later it was owned by a Mr Turner who lived there with his daughter and one of his sons. Mr Turner had an allotment/smallholding at the top of Chapel Hill and every day would pass our house, sometimes pushing a wheelbarrow, and always whistling the same tune – 'Now is the Hour' – a New Zealand song popularised in the UK

Dolly Bliss with Alan's mother – right

by Gracie Fields. Eventually, after the death of old Mr Turner, the son and daughter lived on in the house. The daughter used to play the organ at the chapel and I think that she eventually married one of the Dunstan brothers from Greenhill Farm.

On the same side of the road was a cottage, now called Bliss Cottage (25), which was owned by Alan and Dolly Bliss. Their daughter, Betty, was a year or so younger than me. Alan's mother lived in the small attached cottage.

On the other side of the road were two farm cottages; both were owned by the Finches to house workers at their dairy at the top of Hemplands. The first (26) was occupied by Joe Holland, but later bought from the Finches, in the early 1950s, by a Jewish couple – Mr and Mrs Moier-Williams – who became good family friends of ours. He was a clockmaker/repairer who did contract work for jewellers in Cirencester and Cheltenham. He had a cluttered workshop at the top of the house. Mrs Moier-Williams was an excellent cook and would often bring a plate of Jewish titbits to our door. One of the Finches' cowmen and his wife lived next door (27) with their three sons. One of the sons, Bert Bull, married Monica Juggins, one of Peter Juggins' sisters, and they continued to live on in the cottage. Bert was our scoutmaster at the time.

The Deans lived in York House (29) just a bit further up the road; this building was once a brewery/alehouse. The Deans came from the north of England and, according to my mother, Mr Dean had mental problems which caused embarrassment to his wealthy family. Olive was paid a healthy income to marry him and move away to a remote area of the Cotswolds. To me, Mr Dean was just a bit eccentric; he was a good portrait photographer and had a studio with a darkroom in one of the attics in York House. He did several portraits of us during our childhood. Mrs Dean, although of a stern character, was a good family friend and got on well with my grandmother.

Colin and me (taken in Mr Dean's studio)

Rose Cottage – circa 1908

Opposite York House is a plot of land on which a house named Rose Cottage (28) once stood. In 1929 it was bought by Henry Ford through various third parties, dismantled, shipped to the United States and rebuilt in his open-air museum at Dearborn, Michigan. Nobody spoke of it while I lived in Chedworth and I did not learn about it until recent years; it is almost as if there had been a collective guilt about not having done more to prevent its removal.

Next, up the road on the right was Denfurlong House (31). This was occupied for a while by the Keeling family who became good friends of ours. I seem to remember my parents telling me that Bill Keeling had had a flourishing pie-manufacturing business in the north of England, but Wall's moved in, undercut him and sold to all his outlets. He became bankrupt and moved down to the Cotswolds where he did carpentry work for various building firms. When the Keelings moved to Fossebridge, Denfurlong House was bought by the Baker family.

Rose Cottage Transplanted

In early 1929 Henry Ford appointed Herbert Morton, one of his UK employees, as his agent to anonymously find and acquire a picturesque old-world Cotswold cottage for his museum in Dearborn near Detroit. After a lengthy search for a suitable property, Rose Cottage in Chedworth was found. It was for sale and had all the required features of stone doorways, mullioned windows etc. It was purchased later that year and then extensively renovated before being dismantled. The mason and carpenter involved in taking down the cottage then went to Dearborn to supervise the re-erection. The stones, when labelled and packed, filled over 700 sacks and cases, weighed almost 500 tons and required 68 railway wagons for transport to London docks. There were some architectural changes and some compromise on techniques in reconstruction but every effort was made to recreate the building right down to lime and horsehair plaster. However, people who have visited Dearborn since claim that it has been rendered over-picturesque. At the time, there was a certain amount of controversy surrounding the removal of the building, both locally and nationally including questions raised in Parliament.

On the left at the top of Bleakmore Hill was a lane which, after crossing the railway, led up to Fields Road. On the junction with Bleakmore, a cottage now called Emma's Cottage (33), was occupied by the Carman family. Joe and Emma Carman had five children and the youngest, Alf, was employed in 1946 by my father to help build Grey Gables. As a result of this liaison Alf and his wife Joyce became great friends of the family. Alf went on to drive buses for Harvey's and did the school run to Northleach, and then, in the 1950s, became landlord of the Packhorse Inn in Ampney St. Peter near Cirencester. Alf's older brother Vincent had been killed in a tragic road accident in 1931. On the other side of the road, Green Lane ran down to the bottom of the valley, forded the stream and then carried on up to Greenhill Farm. Mr Fry, a local hurdle maker, lived down the lane; he was captain of Chedworth Cricket Club. Percy Bold, who lived further down, maintained several steam traction engines and also the threshing machine belonging to Gilbert Guest.

The village population was fairly stable and peaceful, with only occasional disputes and grudges. Of course everyone knew each other's business, and rumours and gossip abounded – especially around the unattached. Even today, I remember with some embarrassment how we used to tease Miss Hudman – one of our teachers – about an alleged affair with a local farmer, until she became flustered and her face reddened.

A Fatal Accident on Bleakmore

On 7 October 1930, Vincent Carman (known locally as Vin), aged twenty-one, was killed while returning from work in Cirencester on his motorcycle. He was almost home when he collided with a car, driven by his close friend Joan Milford, on Bleakmore Hill. They had known each other for some years; she had helped him to buy his motorbike and to get his job with the estate agents Hobbs and Chambers – in fact they were probably more than just friends. Joan was driving her Austin Seven in the opposite direction when the collision occurred. Vin received severe head injuries from which he died in Cirencester Memorial Hospital later that day while Joan, although her car turned over, was not badly injured. A verdict of accidental death was subsequently returned.

Martin, me, Colin and Gail – c1948

Gail, Dad, Mum and Colin – c1956

12

Country Childhood

Chedworth was, in those days, a rather remote village in the Cotswolds, and perhaps because of the elevation and the aspect of the Cotswold escarpment the seasons seemed exaggerated, leading to an increased awareness of the changing year.

The countryside was our playground and was idyllic for two young boys. During our school holidays, we would leave the house after breakfast and our mother would not expect to see us again until hunger drove us home towards teatime. We would roam the lanes and woods for miles or dam and fish the local stream. If the weather was particularly hot we would take a picnic and bathe in the river Coln near Fossebridge where the Americans had created a pool by building a dam out of branches and stones.

In spring and early summer the countryside became green and lush. Hawthorn trees were covered with clusters of creamy-white blossom, cow parsley sprouted high by the roadside bearing great branches of sickly-smelling flowers and clouds of elder blossom banked up in the hedgerows. Bees hummed and butterflies flickered among the wild flowers and tangled brambles. The grasses grew up with a rush and almost met across the width of footpaths and lanes, and walking across fields golden with buttercups and cowslips heavy with nectar left our shoes coated with yellow pollen. On warm days lizards would emerge from crevices in the stone walls to soak up the sun and slow-worms could be found curled up in the grass below.

Chedworth Stream

Mum and me in the river Coln

Marsh Marigold (King Cup)

Flag Iris

Cow Parsley

Sticklebacks and minnows darted about in the stream and the marshy areas would be fringed with dense reeds, flag irises, yellow kingcups and wild mint. A dragonfly would hover, vibrating and iridescent over the water and pond skaters flittered across the surface, exploiting the surface tension of the water with their hairy legs. Rafts of frogspawn floated on the surface and bubbles of marsh gas would rise from the mud when disturbed by wellington boots; these bubbles would give a satisfying pop when exposed to a lighted match.

If we were hanging around Greenhill Farm, Jim Dunstan might allow us to ride with him on his tractor or we would get to bottle-feed an orphan lamb. Sometimes we followed a flock of sheep, with a shepherd, as they were moved to spring pastures (the transhumance). This could be for quite a distance around the lanes and back roads of the village. Once we found ourselves out towards Yanworth, about two miles north of Chedworth, and had no idea where we were. The shepherd pointed us in the right direction for home, but we felt quite lost until we began to see familiar landmarks and could make our way back via Horses Ash Lane.

In late summer and early autumn, fields of wheat would rustle in a light breeze and shimmer under the heat of the sun. The fields were dotted with poppies and fringed with wild flowers including vetch, marguerite, cornflowers and the blue and purple meadow cranesbill. The mud of the winter lanes now became a thick white dust which lifted in eddies around the walker's feet. At this time we might help with the local harvest. In late autumn into winter, tangled vines of old man's beard scrambled through the hedgerows and trees along the lanes, topped by silky-grey tufted balls.

Field Poppy

Meadow Cranesbill

One of the highlights of the year was the autumn Harvest Festival held at the Congregational Chapel above Lower Chedworth. The abundance of the countryside was on display and our Sunday School teacher had even tried to lick us into some sort of choir. We would sing lustily, if not tunefully, 'We Plough the Fields and Scatter.'

Congregational Church

A Congregational church is an independent church administered by its congregation and maintains that each member has direct access to God and is directly answerable to Him, not to some individual or organisation that is part of a church hierarchy. The Congregational minister is regarded as 'the first among equals' and is there to serve the members, not to have authority over them. The Congregational method is found in many Baptist and non-denominational churches.

The Congregational Chapel

Children were sent to Sunday School cleaned up and tidy, not, I think, because of any religious beliefs but to give their parents a break after Sunday dinner to laze in peace and quiet through the long afternoon. Post-war, the Chapel still had a significant congregation.

Our country childhood was not always a bucolic ideal, as for example in autumn, when an itinerant slaughter man would come to the village. Mr Petrie, a near neighbour of ours at the top of Pancake Hill, kept a pig and we knew by the squeals when the slaughter man was there. Morbid curiosity would bring several local boys running. It was a cruel and gruesome sight but no attempt was made to disperse the semicircle of gawking boys. Perhaps the spectacle was considered part of our education? However, the business was soon over: the pig gutted, bristles scorched off over a straw fire, the carcass butchered and the hams hung from beams ready for curing. Unlike some of today's children, at least we knew where our food came from.

In winter the south-east orientation of the valley was a funnel for cold, bullying winds from the east. However, the high Cotswolds also gave us ample snow for recreation. The slope behind Grey Gables was excellent for tobogganing – as long as frozen molehills were avoided, as the more daring found to their cost. The low-lying valley bottoms would often flood and freeze over with thick ice. Those of us without skates would work up a slide across the surface, starting from higher and higher up the slope of the hill and racing further and further out across the ice.

Walking through the village during the dark evenings, perhaps on the way to a scout meeting, could be scary or magical. High in the Cotswolds, on a clear night, with no artificial light, the canopy of stars could be breathtaking. One could see the way easily, even if there was no moon. At certain times of the year fireflies would leap from the grass or glow-worms shine in the verges with a lemon fire. However, if the skies were overcast, it could be like walking into a black void; suddenly a fox would bark up in Hedgley Grove, or a cow cough, or horse snort on the other side of the hedge to make you jump out of your skin! Batteries were expensive, and so we learned to do without torches much of the time. A favourite trick was to extend the life of the battery by placing it in a warm oven for a while – this would also warm the hands on a cold night.

The disused wartime airfield was a great source of interest and opportunity for exploration with its control tower and other buildings, some deep within Withington Woods. There was also the quarry, adjacent to Finch's (Denfurlong) dairy farm, which was created to supply the foundation material for the airfield runways, taxiways and aircraft stands.

As children, the railway was a great attraction to us. We might visit the signal box at Fosse Cross station which controlled a passing point on the single track line and also sidings for the limekiln and quarry there. If we were lucky a driver would take us up onto the footplate while they shunted wagons around. We discovered a structure built into the railway embankment, which could have been for wartime defence, and made it our den for a while. From here we would place pennies on the line and retrieve the distorted remains after a train had passed. Eventually, we were warned off by railway workers who were passing on their motorised trolley.

There was a tunnel to the north of the village and one day, while exploring in Chedworth Woods, we found ourselves at its northern portal. Our cousin, Martin, was with Colin and me. After some consideration, Martin and I thought we might try walking through the tunnel. Colin, who had a vivid imagination and was afraid of the dark, was very unhappy about the idea and opted to find his way over the top and meet us at the other end. We waited until a train had come through from the Fosse Cross direction before entering. The tunnel is almost a third of a mile long. However, I knew that, should a train come along, there were probably refuges – recesses in the tunnel wall – for use by railway workers. As we made our way through it got darker and difficult to see the track – the far portal seemed like a small light in the distance. A dank, sooty smell emanated from the walls and, at one point, water streamed down the walls into a channel along the tunnel wall – this must have been the spring which I had heard about. Eventually we emerged from the southern end into bright sunlight and the scent of wild herbs, and climbed the embankment where Colin was waiting. No sooner had we got to the top of the embankment than a goods train came rumbling through, emerging in clouds of steam and smoke!

Today, part of the old route north of Chedworth is a nature reserve and the tunnel is now a home to several species of bats.

The South Portal

13

Village School

St. Andrew's School was probably typical of most village schools at that time. It had three classes with three teachers. Ivor Bowen (the 'Gaffer') was the headmaster, Miss Hudman took the middle class and Miss Irving was the infant teacher. Mr Bowen did his best to instil a basic education into the heads of a mixed bag of country children. Learning was by rote with times tables, spelling bees and writing repeated lines of letters and words. However, country children, as a whole, were not great readers; family life centred around productive gardening, firewood, agricultural activities and other necessary routines. Reading was often considered a waste of time and village gossip might take the place of books, providing a living day-to-day drama. Unfortunately, in those days, children who fell behind were not given much extra help and languished at the back of the class, or were given duties which today would have been carried out by a caretaker. I probably had an advantage as, encouraged by my grandfather, I was already beginning to recognise words when I entered the infants' class. Bullying was common and, because I was shy and had a slight build, I was often on the receiving end. However, I soon learnt to sense when the known bullies were looking for entertainment and would melt out of the way into the background.

As a Church of England school, every day, after assembly, there would be prayers followed by half to three quarters of an hour of religious studies – usually Bible reading or learning a hymn or psalm. On major religious

St. Andrew's Church – Twelfth Century

celebrations the entire school was marched, crocodile-style, to a service at St. Andrew's Church about half a mile away, although there were always some dawdlers whose interest would be diverted.

The school had no running water, no electricity, and outside enclosures housed bucket-type lavatories. The boys' lavatory also boasted an odorous urinal which was just a pitch-painted wall, with a gutter and drain at its base. There was no washing water in the lavatories and the lack of drinking water meant that children had to wait until dinner time, in the adjacent village hall, to slake their thirst, although milk and straws were distributed during the morning. Accidents had to be treated in the schoolhouse where well water was available. Outside there was a large galvanised rainwater tank but this was only suitable for mixing paint or filling vases.

A coal fire heated the infants' room, while the big room, which was divided in two by a folding partition of glass and wood, was heated by a large cast-iron, coke-burning stove. The fires were tended by one of the stouter, older boys and the stove would take a scuttle-full of coke at a time

into its rattling maw. This stove was the focus of our attention between lessons. It gave off pungent, sulphurous fumes and in the coldest weather the top of the stove would glow dull red. If you spat on the top, the spit would hop and gambol across the surface like flies on a windowpane. When the school milk froze, it was placed close to the stove to thaw. In wet or snowy weather, scarves and wet gloves, often soaked through by snowballing, were hung on the surrounding rail to dry and the dank steam from these added to the general fug of the stove and the odours brought by village children. Wet socks and shoes/boots might also line the fireguard. On particularly snowy days, attendance would fall to just a handful of children. In the winter of 1947 the school closed for several days at the end of January, as the roads were impassable; even after this, attendance remained low until mid March.

The big room contained heavy lift-top desks with deeply scored surfaces. Each desk had an inkwell and after dipping our pens we would scratch and blob the ink across our labours. The pupils came from miles around and from many backgrounds: from boys and girls in old boots and ragged clothing from remote farms and cottages to the children of the slightly better-off local artisans and traders. A nurse would call periodically to inspect heads for nits and keep an eye open for other infections. Worms, scabies and food deficiencies could be found, and not just among the poorer children.

The walk to the school, from Amphlett House, was just under one mile each way, in all weathers, and for at least seven months of the year we boys wore stout boots. These were steel-tipped and we could strike sparks from the road surface as we walked. During the walk home in the afternoon we would tend to dawdle, sometimes taking to paths across fields and over stone stiles, searching for hazelnuts, wild strawberries in the grass verges, peeling sour-tasting beechnuts and, of course, gorging ourselves on autumn blackberries; even sloes and damsons, powdered with a blue bloom, could be on the menu – although sloes usually tended to be too bitter.

The school dinner was prepared and served in the adjacent village hall – known as 'The Hut'. This was a rambling, corrugated-iron building which served all the needs of a village hall. It was a place where people voted, where men in suits gathered for meetings, where we sat our eleven-plus exams and where we were sent every week to collect our free orange juice and cod liver oil. It was used for the Christmas pantomime and children's parties, and was occasionally a cinema. Dr Coffey held his weekly surgery there – Dr Coffey's practice, with Dr Gladstone, was based in Rendcomb, near Cirencester. The hut had a characteristic smell, which could only be described as a mixture of boiled cabbage, yellow carbolic soap and dusty floorboards. In very hot weather the inside became stiflingly hot and in cold weather the smelly oil stoves were less than adequate. I did not enjoy the school dinners here, although I am sure the cook did her best in view of post-war shortages. Stew, which seemed to be the standard fare, contained a lot of fat and gristle and was invariably served with mashed swede. Pudding alternated between pink semolina and 'jam tart'. This latter consisted of a slab of soggy lard-based pastry, about half an inch thick, topped with a smear of something red. I suffered from mild acidosis at that time and found it impossible to eat this. I remember on one occasion being kept behind – "until you have finished your pudding". It was not until it was obvious that I was going to be physically sick that I was allowed to return to the playground. Since that time I have never been keen on fatty meat, milk puddings and only in the last few years have come to appreciate swede mashed with butter.

On one memorable occasion, a consignment of food parcels arrived at the school from the American Care Programme. These were divided, rather sparsely, among the pupils; some had personal letters from American families. Luxuries such as tinned apricots were carried home, but a lot of dried goods, such as sultanas, raisins and cornflakes, were devoured on the walk home – Mother may have suspected that there should have been more but didn't say anything!

In 1951, when my brother Colin was nine and I was eleven, we had our first trip, of any distance, beyond the Cotswolds – a school outing to London to the Festival of Britain. It was certainly an adventure for us, but I think a trip to London was also a bit of a novelty for the 'Gaffer'. At one point Colin got lost and separated from the party. He was eventually found in the Dome of Discovery staring open-mouthed at a television – a new experience for a child from a remote village, which only got electricity in 1947. As usual I felt a bit of responsibility for him, but with only one teacher in charge, no one could watch him all the time.

Later Mr Bowen tried to explain the concept of the centre of gravity to us by balancing a pencil on its end; this, he said, was the reason why the Festival Skylon only required light wires to hold it in a vertical position. Mr Bowen's pleasure was obvious whenever he got any sort of intelligent response from his pupils. I had been following the Korean War in our newspaper at home and was the only one able to identify the country in the atlas he held up to the class. It was Mr Bowen who stimulated my interest in drawing – in particular pen and ink drawings of Cotswold buildings. In order to avoid bullying, I had to learn not to raise my hand to every question and, I think, the 'Gaffer' felt some sympathy for this and avoided looking in my direction to enlighten the class.

Uncle Teddy also had a big influence on me and during two summer holidays, probably when I was between eight and eleven, I went to stay with him, 'Aunty' Margaret and their two daughters in Bridgwater. On the first visit, he showed me round his grammar school including its workshops and laboratories – I think the idea was to encourage me to work hard towards the eleven-plus. He was a bit of a stargazer and introduced me to a reflecting telescope he owned. He also borrowed a microscope from the school and suggested things that I should study under its lens. He encouraged me with my reading, steering me to 'quality' books such as Arthur Ransome's *Swallows and Amazons*. On the second visit Colin was invited as well – I think Uncle Teddy and Aunty Margaret regretted it! At the school, while Uncle Teddy was seeing to paperwork in his office, Colin made first for the canteen in search of food (finding only stale biscuits). Then he made his way to the projection room behind the assembly hall, where he opened a can of film – probably the official school film – and managed to unspool the film onto the floor. Uncle Teddy found us both desperately trying to stuff the spool of film back into the can! While there, we were given their daughters' bedroom while they were away staying with friends. Aunty Margaret would bring us a glass of orange juice and an apple every morning. Colin didn't fancy the apples and stuffed them into a drawer between the beds. On the last day, on returning home, one of the daughters came down the stairs and exclaimed, "Mummy, a drawer in our bedroom has a lot of apples in it!"

From a village school that thought it was doing well if one or two pupils a year passed the eleven-plus, Gail, Colin and I all gained entrance to Westwood's Grammar School in Northleach – the same school attended by our parents.

14

Farming Life

Because of petrol shortages during and after the Second World War, horses were still extensively used on farms; however, by then most farmers had at least one tractor. As well as chickens, some villagers still kept a pig in a pigsty feeding them on potatoes and other kitchen scraps.

Living in a country village, we were very aware of farming activity around us, especially at harvest time. If we hung around the fields we were expected to pull our weight – unpaid. This was not child labour, it was the way things were; whole families would be out in the fields helping.

The reaping machine (cutter/binder) was pulled by either two horses or a tractor. It had large rotating paddles which pressed the stalks against the cutters. The wheat then fell onto a belt which fed the binder. We followed the reaper and as the sheaves came off a belt at the back we would pick them up and form them into stooks to dry, nine to twelve sheaves to a stook.

As the area of uncut wheat diminished, farm hands and youths would form a ring around the uncut area holding stout sticks. Soon the rabbits would bolt out, all at once, and those with quick reactions would have rabbit for tea.

After a period of drying, weather permitting, a cart would go from stook to stook to collect the sheaves. Farm hands would pitch the sheaves up onto the cart, where youths and boys were expected to catch and stack them. There was an art to stacking in order to produce a stable load. As boys we were shouted at if we didn't stack in the right way – we soon learnt – and as the load grew so did our height above the ground.

Rabbiting

Then the big day arrived when the threshing machine was set up in the corner of a field. A long canvas belt ran from the power take-off of a tractor to the threshing machine. The sheaves were either tossed up directly from a cart, or a powered elevator took them up to the top of the machine where a man fed them into a hopper. The whole machine was a complex of pulleys, belts and oscillating sieve racks. To a boy, the motion and noise of all the machinery was awesome with the whole operation enveloped in clouds of dust. This was one task in which boys did not take part and were kept well clear of all the machinery. There was some satisfaction in seeing the grain sacks slowly fill at the side of the threshing machine. There would be many farm hands present and families would arrive with refreshments and set up picnics among bundles of sheaves, although harvest mites and other insects could be a nuisance.

The Threshing Machine

Gilbert Guest, from Coln Rogers, owned and hired out a threshing machine. It was taken from farm to farm during the harvest season. Before the war it was powered by a steam traction engine. Percy Bold, who lived down Green Lane from Bleakmore, was the driver and mechanic for the machinery. Percy Bold's daughter, Alma, married Gilbert Guest. After the war, a tractor was used to tow and power the threshing machine.

.Haymaking required dry weather for cutting and turning to dry, and for rick making. A cart loaded with hay was much heavier than when loaded with straw and some of the fields were on steepish slopes. Loading started at the top of a field, and as the cart grew heavier, would require wheel chocks to prevent the load overwhelming the horses. The ricks were used for fodder during the winter and when the time came to dismantle the final few feet of the stack, farm workers and locals would circle the stack with sticks and ratting terriers. As with rabbits during harvest, the rats would break cover all at once. The dogs were much faster than the men and would soon dispose of the rats with a quick shake of the head.

Once a year, in the late autumn, the school closed for potato-picking day. This was not as pleasant a task as the grain harvest. If the day was cold and the ground wet it could be a dirty, miserable job scrabbling in the damp earth for muddy potatoes which had been exposed by the tines of the farmer's tractor; all for a couple of shillings at the end of the day. My mother was not keen on us taking part and so sometimes we would just have the day off.

15

Tobacco and Fireworks

One day, probably in the late 1940s, Dadan decided that he would grow his own tobacco; this may have been prompted by post-war shortages, to save money or simply as a hobby. In any case, young tobacco plants were set out in the back garden adjacent to the ruined cottage; new varieties were available by then, more suited to the British climate. These soon grew into fairly tall plants. In the meantime he built two presses and a guillotine in oak. The compression screws and other metal parts came from Mr Crump – the blacksmith at Fossebridge. As the leaves at the bottom of the plants began to change colour to golden brown, they were plucked off and strung on wires. They were first dunked into the bath in the attic to wash out the strongest undesirable substances and then drained. These lines of leaves were hung across the attic and as they dried began to resemble strings of kippers. When they were completely dry, Dadan would layer them up in the press. After a few layers he would sprinkle them with a solution containing glycerin, honey and saltpetre which was added to keep the cigarette or pipe tobacco burning. Other ingredients such as vanilla might be added for aroma and flavour. Every few days the press screw was tightened and after a week or two a block of tobacco was removed which looked something like a slab of dark brown chipboard. The slab was then shredded in the guillotine to produce tobacco suitable for pipe or cigarettes.

Nicotiana tabacum

On occasions when my cousin Martin was staying at Amphlett House he would be accommodated in the attic. However, he would complain that he could not sleep happily because of the astringent smell of the leaves and that in the semi-darkness the drying leaves looked like bats hanging from the ceiling. While Martin stayed at Amphlett House he took an interest in the growing and processing of tobacco and Daden, in his patient way, explained most of the process. Martin was about nine years old at the time, and during a stay with his other grandparents in Withington, he noticed a man tending a plot of tobacco plants. After exchanging pleasantries, he said to the man, "You should be removing the side shoots and taking off the lower leaves to produce a clean plant." The fellow was impressed and admitted that this was his first try at tobacco growing. Martin then told him to pick the leaves when they are golden and pull off easily, and went on to describe the whole procedure for curing and processing of the product, including the ingredients of the saltpetre mixture. The man thanked Martin for the information and carried on with his hoeing. The next day there was a knock at the front door and Martin's father went to answer it. He returned, with a grave face and said to Martin, "There's a man at the door would like a word with you." Full of trepidation he went to the front door and there stood 'tobacco man' with a smile on his face. "I felt I should reward you for your expert advice," he said, and handed Martin a very large bar of chocolate.

Dadan was quite proud of his home-made tobacco. Earlier I had sent away to a novelty company for some exploding cigarette devices. These looked like small paper torpedoes which could be carefully inserted into a cigarette and sounded like a Christmas cracker when they went off. I had already tried them quite successfully on my father's rolled cigarettes and decided it was time that Dadan began to question the composition of his product. I found his silver cigarette case and, taking one from the middle, primed it with one of the devices and carefully returned it to the case. An hour or so later John Scotford, our neighbour from across the road (5) came to see Dadan. As they were chatting, Dadan lit a cigarette and offered one to Mr Scotford. I watched anxiously as his hand hovered over the case. No not that one, please not that one, I thought – oh no, he's taken it. As Dadan offered him a light, I thought it was time to make myself scarce; however,

Mr Scotford put it behind his ear and said he would save it for later and enjoy it while he was listening to the wireless that evening. He never said anything, but then he didn't ever compliment Dadan on the quality of his tobacco!

While browsing one of Dadan's reference books I came across the formula for gunpowder. I knew I could take a little saltpetre from the large carton he used for tobacco-making, charcoal I could take from partly burnt wood where the bonfire was lit, but where to get sulphur? My grandmother always indulged me and kept my secrets, and so I consulted her. "Well dear," she said, "it's used as an antiseptic and preservative, and can be bought in Boots; I'll get you some next time I'm in Cirencester." A few days later, as she got off the bus, she winked and handed me a box of sulphur – I was in business. At first the mixture did not burn well – more like a Roman Candle – I was looking for something a little more exciting. Eventually I realised that it was necessary to grind and mix the ingredients well and then pack the mixture hard into the cardboard tube; this produced much more dramatic results, although never as explosive as a banger. I tried adding metal filings for sparkle or salts from my chemistry set for colour (e.g. strontium for red or sodium for yellow).

My experiments extended to household chemicals, many of which were freely available in the past but are now strictly regulated and controlled. Even after regulation old products could be found in medicine cabinets and garden sheds.

One day, while exploring the shelves of an outhouse, I came across an old carbide bicycle lamp and a tin of calcium carbide. After playing around with the lamp for a while, I experimented with carbide and water mixtures which usually resulted in fairly gentle detonations like large pops. Potassium permanganate (used for wounds and dermatitis) was much more interesting – a small amount with glycerine added would, after a short delay, flare violently with a purple flame and a mushroom cloud of purple smoke would shoot upwards. Spirits of salt (hydrochloric acid), used as a soldering flux, also provided interesting opportunities – especially in combination with French chalk. Fortunately, I never came to any harm, except occasionally for ringing ears and bright spots before the eyes.

I also experimented with more conventional fireworks. Towards the end of October, children would do all the usual things with bangers, which were much more powerful in those days and could be bought by children of just about any age. However, I wanted to emulate *The Dam Busters* film which had recently been released starring Richard Todd and Michael Redgrave. I built a dam across the stream, then tied several bangers together with a stone. I lit them and held on to them until the primary charge was burning well then dropped the bundle into the deeper water just behind the dam. There was a satisfying muffled thump and large, smoky bubbles rose to the surface, but the dam held. Next I pressed a tight row of bangers into the mud behind the dam wall – this produced the desired effect – the dam was breached and a surge of water ran down the stream bed. Some years later my physics teacher, who was a bit of a maverick, taught us some other tricks with fireworks such as improving the performance of a rocket by launching it from inside a tube or carrying bangers up on a rocket to explode above the school playing field, on one occasion severely disrupting a girls' hockey match.

Cornflower

16

Not Just a Carpenter

After finishing his apprenticeship at Cavendish House, and before the outbreak of the Second World War, my father took a job as estate carpenter at a country estate near Windrush, close to Bourton-on-the-Water. He volunteered early, before the outbreak of the war, and so was able to join the Royal Engineers where his training extended his skills to those that enabled an army to live, move and fight. My father was very resourceful and clever with his hands. I remember him bringing me hand-made toys during his early service leaves, including an elaborately made model Jeep complete with rubber tyres and canvas top. At this time he also made an intricately carved regimental badge, in hardwood and about eighteen inches in diameter. It hung on the wall in every one of our houses and eventually, after both of my parents had died, I donated it to Gibraltar Barracks which is the RE training HQ at Minley, Hampshire. My father enjoyed rapid wartime promotion and eventually rose to the rank of captain before being posted to Burma.

Following his return to Chedworth, I remember traipsing round local farms with him while he repaired farm gates and barn doors; I think the farmers had been asked to provide work to returning servicemen.

The far paddock belonging to Amphlett House was made over to my parents by my grandfather and soon my father had drawn up the plans and the site was laid out for Grey Gables. The building work was started in the spring of 1946 and was completed by late 1947. His building techniques

were up to date and innovative. For example, instead of a conventional first floor of joists and floorboards, he laid a six-inch concrete raft on steel mesh. Fine at the time, but it did present problems for subsequent owners who wanted to extend wiring and plumbing between floors. He installed Crittall metal windows instead of traditional wood, used a flue system which ducted warm air around the fireplaces and up into the bedrooms, and fitted fireproof concrete liners to the chimneys. In all the time we lived there, we never had a chimney sweep; when soot began to fall into the fireplace, Dad would pile

newspapers onto the fire to promote a fire in the chimney and burn out the soot that way – much to the consternation of our neighbours!

Dad had enlisted the help of a local man named Alf Carman who lived with his parents on Bleakmore (33) and was the youngest of five children. Following the completion of Grey Gables, Alf and his wife Joyce remained firm family friends for many years.

After settling in to Grey Gables (now called Springfield) he started a small building firm with his brother Norman who lived in Cheltenham. Uncle Norman had been a prisoner of war and his health was not good following his release; however, he was a good plumber and had a better business head than my father. They built a number of houses before the firm folded after a year or two. Then for several years my father ran a carpentry workshop at Mustows, a building firm in Northleach. Initially he cycled the five miles or so to and from Northleach. He also did carpentry work at home for several local builders. His speciality was staircases which were made using Parana pine – a reddish wood, straight-grained and very strong. He used hand tools at first but soon equipped his workshop with power saws, a planer and a router for cutting the grooves to accommodate the treads and risers.

Cycling to Northleach every day was proving very arduous, especially in winter. Finally, one winter morning he hit a patch of ice going down Hensons Hill towards Fossebridge and suffered a bad tumble, lacerating both his face and hands. Buying even a modest second-hand car at that time would have been financially difficult for the family; however, he did manage to get hold of a vehicle of sorts: it was a 1936 BSA three-wheeler which was a car of unusual design, with a 1000cc air-cooled V-twin engine and front-wheel drive – a feature not generally adopted in cars for many years. The braking was poor and relied on a single front drum brake, whose efficiency was reduced by oil leaking from the adjacent differential. An ineffective handbrake operated on the rear wheel. It was in a poor state when he acquired it and had to be stripped down and rebuilt from scratch. He cleaned and painted the chassis, had the cylinders re-bored and fitted resized pistons. He rebuilt the hardwood frame and beat new body panels from sheets of aluminium alloy. Using my mother's hand sewing machine, he made a new canvas hood. The repainted bonnet was held in place by a leather strap.

My Uncle Chris needed temporary accommodation before he emigrated to Canada with Phyllis, his new wife. They stayed with us at Grey Gables for a while but the situation soon became fraught and stressful, so my father rebuilt an old caravan for them to live in. They had to strip out the interior and completely refit it and a lot of the bodywork needed renovation.

Television sets were few and far between at that time and were beyond the means of most families. However, there was always a copy of *Exchange and Mart* in the house and one day my father spotted an advertisement for war surplus radar sets – 'includes complete instructions for conversion to a television set'. He sent for one! The cathode ray tube was six inches in diameter and about two feet long. The chassis was massive, with valves up to six inches high on top, alongside large metal-encased capacitors. Vane capacitors driven by long rods and bevel gears were connected to knobs on the front. Underneath, the resistors were as large as AA batteries and waxed capacitors looked like oversized toffees. The conversion instructions were sketchy to say the least! Anyway, the carpenter, with no knowledge of electronics, persevered. He had two soldering irons – one in use and the other thrust into the fire heating up. The winter evenings were filled with the smell of soldering flux as he stripped and rewired it to receive a TV signal with sound channel and to provide suitable voltage drives to the large coils on the rear of the CRT. Eventually, after a lot of trial and error, a rectangular TV 'raster' appeared on the screen and with further tweaking a ghostly picture appeared. It was ready just in time to see the funeral of King George VI on 15 February 1952. We could just about make out what we supposed were horses and the coffin on a gun carriage. Dad made a handsome mahogany cabinet for it and gave it pride of place in the living room to the right of the fireplace. The picture was rather unstable and tended to flip horizontally or vertically so it was necessary to keep getting up and making fine adjustments to controls behind the set.

One day, during school assembly, probably in May the following year, Mr Bowen asked if all those with televisions at home could raise their hands. There were two, or perhaps three, including my brother, who did. Mr Bowen divided all of the assembly into groups and allocated one group to each house having a set, ready for Coronation Day on 3 June. When Colin got home and told my father, he was furious – "I don't want a load of village children in my house on Coronation Day." On the great day the living room was packed with children and adults, all peering at a blurry image on the distant screen. Dadan, who was sitting at the back, had brought his binoculars to try to improve his view! My sister Gail, who was only five at the time and feeling very nervous, was tasked with passing round trays of tea and sandwiches.

My father had already cancelled his subscription to *Carpenter and Builder* and was taking the *Practical Television* magazine instead. He now started building a new set based on a published design. This was state-of-the-art, with a twelve-inch screen and automatic feedback for picture stabilisation. Valves and other components were much smaller now, and a small electric soldering iron made assembly much easier. He worked carefully, highlighting each part of the circuit diagram as it was completed. It worked almost immediately with only a minor modification provided by a local repair engineer. We marvelled at the quality of the picture – we could actually see smoke rising from the panellists' cigarettes on the *What's My Line?* quiz show.

One summer, probably in 1954, my parents hired a four-berth cabin cruiser on the Thames. We took it downstream from Oxford and although it rained a lot, and the deck leaked through onto our bunks, we all enjoyed it. On our return my father cancelled his subscription to *Practical Television* and took *Motor Boat and Yachting* instead. He soon

found plans for a two-berth cabin cruiser that appealed to him. The garage/workshop at Grey Gables was now quite large and when cleared out and tidied up was large enough to build the boat about 20ft long, although the bow would have to extend through the doors.

Firstly, he made a scale model about two feet long and floated it in the bath to test it for trim and overall balance. Then, to the real thing. The rib frames had to be made first and spaced upside down on a temporary frame. Next he procured a long length of mahogany for the keel. This had to be spliced and curved for the bow and then slotted into the rib frames. Marine ply was then cut to shape and clamped to the curve of the ribs before being screwed/glued into place; brass screws were used throughout the construction. After final shaping and finishing, marine paint was applied to the completed hull; it was now ready for inversion.

He had already bought a war surplus ammunition trailer and with the help of Mr Crump, the blacksmith at Fossebridge, converted it into a boat trailer. They welded a length of steel channel down the centre of the trailer to accommodate the keel. Steel cross-members were then welded on and a wooden cradle was added to support the boat. Several local men were recruited, and on the appointed day, the hull was carefully eased out through

the doors with about an inch to spare on either side. The trailer was then moved into position in the garage, the hull inverted and eased back onto the trailer. The helper on the left of the picture is Arthur (Jock) McNeil, in the centre is Cliff Clark and between them is his lodger at the time, who was a student at the local agricultural college. One of those on the right may be Mr Petrie.

The boat was now ready for fitting out. He bought a second-hand marine engine complete with propeller and shaft – probably through *Exchange and Mart* – and took my sister, Gail, with him to pick it up at Gloucester Dockyard. We scoured the scrapyards around Cirencester for other parts such as a petrol tank and pump, and electrical items. He made a hardwood helm

and a folding canvas cockpit cover which could provide extra accommodation. My mother made curtains, mattress covers and other soft furnishings.

On the great day the boat was launched from the slipway at Lechlade and it floated with no leaks, only needing a bit of ballast for trim. It was christened Skoo, which was a family nickname for my mother. My father had created a local legend in Chedworth by building a boat in the garage of a house which was some distance from any navigable water. Many holidays and day outings followed over the years. Some Sunday afternoons we would just make up a picnic and take the boat a short way downstream from Lechlade and moor under trees for the afternoon.

17

The 1950s and Changing Times

During the 1950s the variety and quality of products, including foodstuffs, gradually improved; in February 1953 confectionery rationing ended and, finally, all rationing was ended in July 1954. National brands disappeared and were replaced by commercial branding. I can remember my mother sending for a free Stork margarine cookery book and she and I must have tried every cake and biscuit recipe in it; mostly the whole family enjoyed the results and many years later the book, worn and falling apart, was still being used. In contrast to the unpalatable school dinners at primary school, I actually enjoyed the meals on starting at Westwood's Grammar School in 1951; the puddings, in particular, were varied and sustaining. At home as well, life became less austere; even so the quality of meat was still not good and the Sunday joint had to be either braised or pot-roasted. Weekly vans started to ply the village: a butcher from Northleach, a travelling library (which my mother and I made full use of) and even an ice cream van. We now could afford to buy the occasional chicken, which was just as well when the post-war staple of rabbit became unavailable in 1954 due to the arrival of myxomatosis. This was a terrible disease; it was pitiful to see the poor creatures blinded by sores and sitting paralysed in the open. Even as children we had to learn to carry heavy sticks and do what was best for them. Soon concerned locals with shotguns began to carry out regular patrols of the area during the evenings.

In about 1950 mains water was installed. This came from an underground source near Bibury and was pumped up the Coln Valley via a series of pumping stations. However, many people still preferred to take water from their wells claiming, perhaps with some justification, that it tasted much better.

In the late 1940s and early 1950s there was a national drive for council house building and Chedworth was not excluded. A stark row of houses was built on Hemplands right on the southern horizon from Lower Chedworth. There was much grumbling by the residents regarding their spoilt rural view. However, post-war, sympathetic rural planning got little consideration. That said, people who lived in a simple cottage with no electricity, running water or sanitation couldn't wait to get into one of these houses with the luxury of a flush toilet and light at the flick of a switch. The rent of thirty shillings a week (subsidised) did cause some complaint after having paid only a few shillings a week for an old cottage. But then the buildings were falling into disrepair as no landlord could keep them in good order for 'three bob a week'. The new tenants certainly enjoyed a fine view, across the valley to the village, while washing up at the kitchen sink.

To catch the school bus we had to walk up Hemplands Hill to Denfurlong Farm on Fields Road. This was a dairy farm and there was always some activity to watch until the bus came. A large bull was kept in an adjacent field. He was a mean fellow and if you got too close to him would lower his head and paw the ground. From time to time he would be brought into an enclosure in the yard and a cow would be brought out for him to serve. He was an experienced operator; his aim was true and he had earned his keep in less than fifteen seconds.

The school bus served both secondary schools in Northleach; from Chedworth the journey took almost an hour, picking up from a number of scattered villages down the Coln Valley: Fossebridge, Coln St. Dennis, Calcot, Coln Rogers, Abingdon to Bibury and then across country to Northleach. The journey was tedious but not without its occasional highlights. In winter, snow often made the going treacherous. At Calcot Peak about halfway between Bibury and Northleach there was a particularly steep hill. Sometimes, having come this far, deep snow and drifting would force the driver to turn round, with much cheering from the pupils, and make his way back to the safer A429 Fosse Way and on to Northleach. My brother Colin always had a good singing voice and could be relied upon to relieve the tedium of the journey with a rendering of the latest Johnny Ray and other hits of the time: 'Jezebel', 'Just Walking In The Rain', 'Green Door'.

Westwood's Grammar School still had some of the same teachers in 1951 when I started as when attended by my parents in the 1930s – including the headmaster Mr Bassett ('The Burf') and Mr Wellman the carpentry teacher. The school was good as far as it went, but lacked in some respects, such as teaching chemistry and music, and had little idea of academic progression – leaving at age sixteen was still the norm. For me the physics teacher, 'Yogi' Crellin, was inspirational. He made the subject interesting, with practical experiments relating to everyday life. Safety had little consideration; on one occasion he tried to measure whether any improvement could be made in the thrust of a model aeroplane 'Jetex' motor by doctoring the propellant with various chemicals – it finally blew apart in front of a startled class. Out of class he demonstrated how to boost the performance of rockets and bangers. He also organised lunchtime films and ran a model aeroplane club.

Gradually the propeller-driven fighter aircraft were seen less often in the skies over Chedworth and were replaced by a new generation of jet fighters; the first of these was the Gloster Meteor, criss-crossing the skies as the pilots got used to the new method of propulsion. Soon the swept-wing aircraft, such as the Hawker Hunter, replaced the Meteor. Often, when sitting in class at school, we would hear the double 'thrump-thrump' as the sound barrier was broken. We would whisper to each other, "Was that the new English Electric Lightning?" to which the reply was probably, "Nah, it's a Yank Super Sabre." A fixed stare from the teacher would immediately quieten us, except in the physics lessons; 'Yogi' Crellin was just as interested as we were and would take it as a cue for a talk on sound transmission and the production of a shock wave.

Fairford had one of the wartime airfields and in 1950, under a Cold War agreement, it was transferred to the USAF for use by the Strategic Air

Command (SAC). The wartime installations needed a lot of upgrading and this provided much-needed work for local people. The runway was extended to 10,000ft and new support facilities were built, including special weapons bunkers. The messes and social facilities could only be described as a 'mini USA'. My father, who was specialising in floor laying by then, got the work for laying a dance floor in the main hall. Helping my father at weekends I had a taste (literally) of the American way of life. The floor was a success, and he even did a large inlay of the SAC emblem (a mailed fist clutching several bolts of lightning). He also did a lot of work on the married quarters at Brize Norton.

During this time he crossed paths with old workmates including his old friend Bill Keeling, who was doing carpentry work at the bases. Soon the giant B-47 Stratojets, with their lethal cargos, were lumbering low over Chedworth as they came in towards Fairford, dragging braking parachutes. These aircraft had six engines and could fly fast, at high altitudes, on their 24/7 Cold War missions.

Gail with model based on the Gloster Javelin all-weather fighter.

Besides Meccano and other hobbies, building model aircraft was my passion, particularly gliders. The steep north-facing slope above Grey Gables often had a favourable updraught and, launched from the top, a glider might soar out over the valley towards the houses opposite or down the valley into Hedgley Bottom. I frequently had to retrieve the craft from somebody's apple tree or race to save it from curious cows.

In our living room the fumes of balsa wood glue and fabric dope were added to those of soldering flux produced by my father's TV construction and, of course, cigarette smoke.

Shortly after starting grammar school, probably in 1952, I was upstairs building something out of Meccano when there was a tremendous bang followed by the rattle of tiles tumbling down the roof – we had been struck by lightning. A hole about one foot in diameter had been blown in the roof, the roofing felt set on fire, a transformer blown out in the television and the TV aerial had melted and was sagging like an image in a Salvador Dali painting. My brother and I had just got over mumps but my father had caught it from us and was seriously indisposed, as adult males are, and confined to bed with a temperature of 105 degrees. However, he got out of bed and went outside, in the pouring rain, to see what the damage was; all of this panic made Mum somewhat hysterical. While Gail tried to calm Mother down, it was left to me to climb up into the smoke-filled loft and dowse the smouldering felt. Later Dad built a new TV aerial from aluminium rods and had me climb up onto the roof and help hold it in place while he clamped it to the chimney.

Most of our recreation, in those days, was home or locally generated with, perhaps, the occasional trip to the cinema in Cheltenham. However, once a year, in October, the Mop Fair came to Cirencester. These fairs used to be hiring forums whereby servants and farm workers put themselves forward for hire. Each person had a badge or external symbol expressive of their occupation. Harvey's would lay on a special bus to take people from Chedworth and surrounding villages to the Mop, which by then was just a funfair. One year I had saved up my pocket money for several weeks and finally had five shillings to spend. One of the amusements was like a giant roulette wheel with the prizes displayed round the edge. My little sister, Gail, had talked about wanting a doll which walked and would close its eyes when laid down; there at the back of the stall was such a doll. I bought a ticket, the wheel spun, then stopped at my number and so I asked for the doll. This is easy, I thought. I already had my eye on something I wanted for myself so I bought another ticket, but this time the wheel failed to stop on my number – there's something wrong with the system, I thought, I'll try again. Soon my five shillings had gone and I had no choice but to trail around after my friends, carrying a large box with a doll in it, until it was time for the return bus. This was an early lesson in probability and I have hardly ever gambled since.

We would often go to classic car events, such as rallies and hill climbs, with the Clark family, who lived opposite us on the other side of the valley in Hill House. During the 1950s, they kept a smallholding with ducks, chickens and pigs, the latter being kept in our paddock. Those pigs were great escapees – we were always having to round them up and drive them out of our garden before they ate all the vegetables. When the Clarks went on holiday I would earn a bit of money looking after the livestock. The ducks and chickens were fairly easy to look after; they even put themselves to bed, and all I had to do was close the hutch door against foxes. However, bacon pigs are large animals and would often knock me over while I was trying to carry heavy buckets of feed to the troughs. I learnt that the best way to do this was to carry a small amount first to keep them occupied and then go back for the bulk of the feed which I had left behind the paddock wall. At the appropriate time Cliff Clark would enlist my help to get one of his 'girls' into a trailer and take her to be served by a boar belonging to a local farmer. Unlike Finch's bull, the boar could be slow and clumsy, and take a lot longer to earn his keep. Sometimes we had to leave the couple overnight to sort things out.

When a sow is coming to term she will start collecting large mouthfuls of grass and building a 'nest' in what she thinks is an appropriate place. On one occasion a sow had been nest-building for a couple of days. The Clarks and my parents had already arranged to go to some motoring event that day, which they really didn't want to miss. Cliff Clark looked at the sow and pronounced that she would be a day or so yet, but could I just keep an eye on her. No sooner had they gone, the sow lay down on her nest and I could sense by her behaviour that something was about to happen. When I got to her she was heaving slightly and her vulva was protruding and swollen. Very soon she gave a heave, gasped, and the first piglet slid out. I was amazed at the energy and vitality of the little fellow. It thrashed and struggled to get around Mum's hind legs, but there was a problem: it was constrained by the umbilical cord, which was still attached within the mother. I wasn't sure what to do so I pulled it gently and it came away fairly easily. I learnt later that this was the correct thing to do – not to cut or break it. The remaining

nine came easily, at regular intervals – one or two of them needing a little help with their direction finding. Later when I went back to check on them, I picked up the afterbirth in a bundle of hay and took it to the far side of the field where I threw it over the wall to distract the crows, which were starting to show an unhealthy interest in proceedings.

The stone walls, characteristic of the Cotswolds and surrounding most of the fields, were very durable but occasionally sections would fall down due to age, the action of weather or the pressure of livestock – particularly pigs and scrambling sheep. Old photos of Lower Chedworth, taken from the other side of the valley, show a small stone-built barn at the top of the upper paddock. By the 1940s this had been demolished and much of the stone used elsewhere; but the foundations remained and, as children, we would build ramparts and other structures of our own design. The uncut stones were of various weights and sizes and mostly irregular, and we soon learnt the skills necessary to juggle and fit them to form well-shaped and stable structures. As a result I soon came to enjoy repairing local walls, and eventually became quite good at it and an asset to the local farmer who could not always get to the scene in time to prevent animals from straying. During

Lower Chedworth in the 1920s showing the old barn in the upper right of the paddock. Below this on the stream is the site of Godbridge Mill which once stood there.

and after the war the state of these walls deteriorated; however, in the late 1950s government grants became available for the repair and renovation of the stone walls and there was a revival of the craft for locals who still had the skills. Without this support it is certain that many landowners would have had to resort to cheaper fencing and hedges and much of the character of the area would have been lost.

Dry Stone Walls

The sides of a Cotswold dry stone wall are constructed with large stones at the base progressing to smaller stones near the top. The central cavity is usually filled with rubble with occasional tie stones across the width of the wall. The sides are angled slightly inwards so that the wall is narrower at the top – professionals use a wooden frame and lines to keep the shape. Finally flat stone 'toppers' are packed vertically along the top for protection and to give stability.

By the early 1950s my grandparents were beginning to find Amphlett House a bit too much for them and then in 1953 my grandfather suffered a stroke and, although he made a fairly good recovery, it was decided that it was time for them to move. My father built a large garage/workshop extension on the side of Grey Gables (where the boat was later built). He then converted the existing integrated garage into a downstairs bedroom. In 1954 Amphlett House was sold and my grandparents moved in with us. Unfortunately, my grandfather died the following year after suffering a second stroke.

As well as improvements in food, services, housing and employment opportunities, there were various other social changes: for example, in ownership of cars and televisions and in the availability of books and newspapers. In particular, there was a revolution in popular music. To a young teenager in the early 1950s, popular music at that time was pretty dire. Topping the charts in 1954 was Doris Day with 'Secret Love'. There were Perry Como, Frank Sinatra ('Three Coins in the Fountain') and Winifred Atwell on her piano. My parents loved it all. If the weather forced us to stay indoors on a Sunday afternoon, the BBC Light Programme would be on and we had to suffer *Family Favourites*, *The Billy Cotton Band Show* and to round off there was *Sing Something Simple* in the early evening. Then, in 1955–56, rock and roll arrived. It hit young people like a thunderbolt and changed popular music forever. It was immediately censored by the BBC. If we were lucky a British Forces Overseas request for Elvis Presley might be played. We did not have a record player, and in any case could not afford to buy records. Our only option was Radio Luxembourg, which was the only station broadcasting pop music at the time. My grandmother had her own radio in her room and in the evenings, if the television was on, I would declare that I had to go into gran's room to do my homework. Ever indulgent, she allowed me to tune in to Radio Luxembourg – not easy as it tended to drift and fade and one was constantly having to fiddle with the tuning dial. When Mrs Dean, who lived in York House (29), bought one of the new FM radios, she gave me her old portable AM set which I kept with me for years until Radio Caroline put an end to the BBC monopoly.

By my mid teens I was looking for holiday and weekend jobs to boost my pocket money. Mrs Dean was a great help and would arrange gardening and carpentry jobs for me around the village. Also Mr Moier-Williams, the Jewish clockmaker, would enlist my help when he had a lot of contract work on. I would dismantle clocks into a tray and then clean all the components. He would then reassemble and lubricate them, complete any repairs and finally regulate them over the next few days.

In 1956 at the age of sixteen I left my home in Chedworth after being offered a job as a laboratory technician at the Royal Military College of Science at Shrivenham, just north of Swindon. I returned to Chedworth most weekends. Until the line closed in 1961, it was possible to get a train from Swindon Old Town to Chedworth; however, the service was infrequent, not at convenient times and, towards the end, you had to remember to ask the guard to halt the train at Chedworth, otherwise, as happened to me on one occasion, I found myself taken straight through to Cheltenham. Normally I either cycled the whole distance – about twenty-two miles – or took a bus from Swindon to Cirencester. In the latter case I walked out of Cirencester to the A429 where I hoped to thumb a lift as far as the Chedworth turn; on at least one occasion I had to walk the whole eight miles in the dark. On one particularly dark night, walking out of Cirencester, I saw a shadowy figure ahead of me on the road; I increased my pace, and as I passed, there was a gasp and the figure lurched backwards in fright. It must have been an old tramp and as I disappeared into the night he must have thought that the devil had come for his soul! On Monday mornings I could get a lift into Cirencester from Jock McNeil – Monday was college day and I only had to get to Swindon in time for the first lecture. As soon as I was seventeen, I acquired a small two-stroke motorcycle (a 'Tandon'), which I learnt to ride on the flat stretch of road above Hensons Hill. I later saved up £60 and bought a 1938 Morris Eight. Like many people in the area I learnt to drive a car on the runways of the old airfield. Sometimes my mother, who had a licence, would accompany me but at other times I removed my L-plates and drove alone up Fields Road to the airfield to practise my reversing and three-point turns on the marked-out areas there.

Me and Martin on the Tandon

My father had now set up a flooring company and was getting most of his work in Wiltshire. As a result, in 1959, they sold Grey Gables and moved to Highworth just north of Swindon where they bought a plot of land on which my father built a bungalow. So ended the family connection with Chedworth and I departed the limited horizons of a Cotswold village, moving further afield, first to the Swindon area and eventually to London and beyond.

They say that there is nothing like staying away for bringing it with you – that is certainly true for my memories of Chedworth.

Greater Knapweed

Lady's Bedstraw

18

An Evolving Village

With time the village changed: TV aerials sprouted from roofs and garden walls were breached to accommodate parking areas and drives. Soon, the first Range Rovers were parked outside the Seven Tuns. Cottages were converted to holiday lets and new infill houses built; these latter, although using Cotswold architectural styles and materials, were sometimes larger and could dwarf the older cottages. Latterly, fast broadband fibre has been laid through the village to the benefit of both residents and local businesses.

My father built Grey Gables in 1946–47, for perhaps a few hundred pounds, using money saved from his wartime service pay. It was subsequently sold in 1959 for about £2,000. Since then the house, renamed Springfield, has been considerably extended, modernised, the garden landscaped and part of the paddock converted into a wild flower meadow. It has recently been on the market for £925,000. When we lived there the house, in spite of all our efforts at home building, was rather austere and the garden very utilitarian. One day in the spring of 2006 my wife and I were showing some friends around the village and after lunch at the Seven Tuns we discovered that, by coincidence, the village had a garden open day and that Springfield was one of the gardens being shown. We were most impressed by the landscaping and the transformation of the house. The owner at that time confirmed that the boat, built in the garage of the house, is still a local legend, as have other people I have spoken to in the village.

When my grandparents left Amphlett House in 1954 it was bought, in January 1955, by Richard and Shelagh Lovett-Turner. Shelagh was still living in the house – over 60 years later – when in June of 2015 we had reason to be travelling up the Fosse Way and decided to have a quick look at the village. Passing Amphlett House we noticed windows open and decided, on impulse, to knock at the door. Shelagh made us most welcome and we sat talking in the old scullery for about two hours exchanging memories of the house and Chedworth. I felt immediately at ease with her as she reminded me so much of my grandmother, who could be quite brusque and intimidating,

Shelagh Lovett-Turner

and frequently outspoken. Perhaps it is something to do with Amphlett House requiring a forceful matriarch? Shelagh gave us the freedom to look round the house and garden and I was really pleased to see how little had been changed, and the changes that had been made were either necessary or in keeping with the character of the house. For example, dormers in the roof to give light to the attic, an opening knocked through to link the main house and cottage attics and central heating installed. In the garden some of the pear trees, which were old when I was there, survive along the north wall. Apparently, the electric pump over the well had been in use until quite recently, when a bad leak in the main pipe down the well put it out of action. In the meantime the house has been connected to the mains water supply. What was the back garden has been separated off and a new cottage (Pancake Cottage) built on the site of the old ruin.

My mother and both of my grandmothers lived to the age of ninety-four; my Gran Pilkington tended her vegetable plot and cooked herself a

Gran Foice in her late 80s

fatty brisket joint every week until almost the end, while my mother and Gran Foice were both lifetime smokers; there are some exceptional people who smoke and yet live to an old age. Gran Foice remained a snob, was outspoken and made pithy comments about people and life in general. I remember that just before I got married I took Carolyn, my wife-to-be, down to Cheltenham to introduce her. Gran, at one point, looked at Carolyn and said, "And where do you come from?" Carolyn replied brightly, "Oh, near Chelmsford in Essex." Gran responded briefly and rather haughtily, "I see." I interrupted and said, "But Gran, after we get married we are moving to Wokingham in Berkshire." Gran brightened and replied, "Ah, that's all right then," – approval was won!

Another long life was that of Doris Hudman, the middle school teacher who subsequently married Harold Andrews, the bus driver. She died only recently, aged over one hundred.

Peter Juggins is now in his late eighties and is still taking commissions for stonemasonry. In 2000 he carved and installed a millennial stone lectern for St. Andrew's Church. He played in the village silver band for seventy-seven years, until quite recently.

The chapel, which was built in 1804, was closed in 1967 and in 1981 was converted into a private dwelling by the present owners. The adjoining annexe/Sunday school has been converted into a holiday let.

Like many farms, those in the village have had to modernise and diversify. Dairy farming at Denfurlong, to the south of Lower Chedworth, ceased and the buildings remained empty for some years until they were converted, by the Finch family, into a farm shop and adjoining cafe, which opened in March 2006. A campsite has been established in the adjacent disused quarry.

Greenhill Farm, to the north of Lower Chedworth, which was owned by the Dunstan family, was acquired by the Stowell Park estate. Combine harvesters were deployed to extend harvesting times and the whine of a grain dryer filled the air, over Lower Chedworth, day and night. The farm has now been converted to livery stables, a riding school and for the use of polo ponies.

Millennial lectern

The Seven Tuns pub closed for more than a year before reopening in May 2015 under new management with a new dining room offering locally sourced food.

The Seven Tuns, Chedworth

The Packhorse Inn, where Alf Carman, the bus driver for Harvey's, and his wife, Joyce, were landlords during the 1950s, is no longer a pub. It is now a private house and their daughter, Myra, still lives there.

The character of the Cotswolds is defined by rolling hills, the limestone quarried there and the distinctive building styles used, in addition to the people and their traditions. Old village photographs always tend to show people walking or standing gossiping in doorways of picturesque cottages. However, it is too easy to idealise the past; the roads were tracks just about sufficient for carts and the cottages were built for farm labourers and local craftsmen; life was hard and the living conditions austere. By the early 1900s many of the cottages were in a poor condition with leaking roofs and damp walls, as well as lacking drainage and adequate water supplies. It is no wonder that moving to a new council house with indoor toilets, running water and an electricity supply was an attractive prospect. At the same time incomers to Chedworth (retirees, second home buyers, holiday let developers or even people running a business from home via the internet) could buy the homes cheaply and restore them, while creating work for local craftsmen. Some of the extensions and new-builds may be somewhat out of proportion to the surrounding cottages. While walking through the village today one sees fewer people and must be constantly stepping on to the verge to let large cars pass. Footpaths and lanes that I remember from childhood have become overgrown and blocked with nettles and tangled brambles. However, although the nature of the village and its occupants may have changed, the valley and the scenery remains, and the vitality of the village has been preserved.

Chedworth is a well-kept secret; it has architecture and scenery to match anything in the Cotswolds but does not suffer hordes of visitors in the summer like Bibury or Bourton-on-the-Water with the consequent tourist coaches, traffic jams and olde worlde tea/souvenir shops. Over the years I have returned – it is a place to which my wife and I like to take visitors, particularly our American friends, with lunch at the Seven Tuns, a walk through the village and, perhaps, finishing up at the Roman Villa.

Dog Rose

Steps

Steps mount to loft, scarce used but hay-, dust-smelling;
Below, valerian, spring leaves, flowers swelling,
Making frame for ancient store –
Tallet, with trap in creaky floor.

Picture – beasts below, food above;
Young, we cousins used to love
Hiding here; with imagining, contrive
To make absent cattle come alive.

For some, older, such steps force one to take
Retirement, and beasts and hay forsake;
Back-break burden of fodder tossed
And herding of beasts to pasture, lost.

Childhood playthings, the stairs and wall;
Lichen-studded, where long weeds fall
In showers to cloak the settling stones;
Was neglect occasioned by once broken bones?

As we played, we little cared or thought
Of those who'd hauled, sweated over stones new-wrought;
Of those who'd rented, bought, and hard depended
On this now ruin, till it, like them, the modern world transcended.

Now folk buy such places to convert
To commuter pads with flower-troughs pert,
Boasting 'village home', twee rustic name,
Unknowing of all before they came.

We of earlier vintage loved it homely – though unkempt,
And treat such usurpation with contempt,
Awaiting a time perhaps when they
Might tire of pretension and slide away.

Will the great wheel of time revolve
For borrowers who cannot debt resolve;
Recycle their ostentation, brashness
And rebuke them for over-mortgaged rashness?

And will people repay their real long-term owing,
Engaging anew in prudent sowing, growing;
And as in man's earlier story, less now told,
Receive interest on their labour manifold?

Martin Kilbey, June 2018

Tallet Steps

The poem on the previous page was written by my cousin Martin and refers to the
Tallet Steps painting above.